Portraits of Poverty

by Edythe Shewbridge

Portraits
of Poverty

W · W · NORTON & COMPANY · INC ·
NEW YORK

FIRST EDITION

Library of Congress Cataloging in Publication Data
Shewbridge, Edythe.
    Portraits of poverty.
    1. Poor—U. S.   2.   Public welfare—U. S.
I. Title.
HV95.S47   362.5'0973   72-1114
ISBN 0-393 01094 5 (Cloth Edition)
ISBN 0-393 01096-1 (Paper Edition)

Published simultaneously in Canada
by George J. McLeod Limited, Toronto

PRINTED IN THE UNITED STATES OF AMERICA

1   2   3   4   5   6   7   8   9   0

Contents

Author's Note

ALL NAMES, addresses, and other identifying data in these case histories have been altered. The content, however, is factually accurate, and based on my own three years of experience as a caseworker with the New York City Department of Social Services.

Acknowledgments

THIS BOOK would not have been written had it not been for the assistance provided by Mrs. Jayne Conrad, who worked tirelessly deciphering my often-illegible typing, and proofreading the manuscript, because she believed that this story should be told.

I owe thanks, which are hereby extended, to Professor Marion Hauk of the University of Virginia, for her helpful comments and criticisms on the first draft of the manuscript. A more restrained and better-organized book is the result.

My mother, Mrs. Doris Shewbridge, earned my gratitude, by giving me unlimited patience and understanding, and by typing all my correspondence.

Portraits of Poverty

ONE

Introduction

I wrote this book to illustrate that, a cultural tradition romanticizing poverty to the contrary, to be poor in a bureaucratized society is not a thing of joy. Nor is the dependency caused by one's poverty a matter of autonomous choice. Particularly is this true when one must depend upon bureaucratic whim for such basic needs as carfare and school clothing.

If the poor are "simple and childish," and incapable of self-government (as opinion within the Department of Social Services and in society at large asserts), perhaps it is the ultimate result of the pervasive double-binds imposed by those agencies empowered by society with the power of life and death over America's poor. These agencies join with society in condemning the dependency of the economic underclass, while offering its individual members no viable alternative to dependency.

As fuctionaries of such agencies, we preach "self-determination" to our clients, while subjecting their most minute requests to exhaustive scrutiny. While our daily rulings and case decisions are strongly influenced by our middle-class standards, our clients' efforts to achieve middle-class comfort and convenience in their own lives are almost inevitably penalized by the curtailment of future funds. While we assume that these clients should be like us in adhering to standards of responsibility and initiative, we restrict access to the facilities and resources (such as higher education, libraries, movies, museums, and family planning information) likely to foster these virtues.

Thus, while we assert that all clients having the potential capacity for self-support should work, the provision of funds for carfare and clothing (without which the process of seeking employment is decidedly handicapped) was recently rescinded by administrative dictate. A working mother who requests the addition of baby-sitting fees to her budget faces a possible delay of up to three months, with no real guarantee of payment even then. Very few babysitters are so altruistic or so well off that they will work without pay (especially if future retroactive payment is not even assured) for this length of time. Adequate day-care facilities (in fact, any facilities at all for the care of children of working mothers) are simply not available to the financially insolvent applicant.

The recipient who attempts to insure his future ability for independent self-support by taking vocational training, or by attending university extension courses, may be penalized by the cessation or denial of present support.

The few jobs located for clients through the Department of Social Services Division of Employment and Rehabilitation almost invariably pay below minimum wage. With no provision for carfare to and from the job, the worker "serviced" by this agency often finds his financial situation worsened by his new employment.

Teachers, school social workers, and employees of the De-

14

partment of Social Services place the blame for the slum child's failure to distinguish himself academically on low parental involvement and motivation. They fail to consider the obvious fact that such simple prerequisites for concentrated study as privacy and freedom from excessive distractions are impossible to provide in the typical welfare apartment. Frequently, two or three children share one bed in a hall corner, with no door separating their sleeping quarters from those of their parents and siblings. Acquisition of new furniture, or permission to move, have been Departmentally forbidden for the past year and a half. Nor are these parents allowed funds for clothing their school children. Indeed, they are lucky if the ninety cents per day allotted for each child's food is consistently provided. When checks are delayed for any reason, these children go without food for days at a time. (Inadequate clothing and empty stomachs are notoriously nonconducive to academic distinction.) Recurring crises such as utility shutoffs, nonreceipt of checks, and accident or injury to other members of the family necessitate the absence of these children from classes. The occasional adolescent who is able to overcome all these obstacles, achieving acceptance by a college or university, may be penalized (along with the other members of his family) by seeing welfare assistance to his parents terminated. The theory is that the aspiring student should go straight to work, regardless of pay, future promotion, or menial task, even though, legally, the student may not be responsible for his parents' support.

While social-work professionals condemn their clients' derelictions from conventional standards of personal hygiene, the physical circumstances of ghetto life make anything approximating adequate health practices an impossibility. The typical welfare apartment is plagued by rodents and bedbugs. While the burning of a light during the nighttime hours may keep these pests away from babies, it results in exorbitant fees to Con Edison, and is not covered by special allowance from the Department of Social Services. The apartments are frequently overcrowded past the legal limit. School children living in these apartments must attend school in winter without coats, gloves, hats, or intact shoes.

The recipient with medical problems must rely on an impossibly overburdened city hospital system for medical care. He receives no allotment for carfare to and from scheduled clinic visits. Either he pays carfare from his ninety-cents-a-day food allowance, or he does without medical care.

The single recipient afflicted with failing eyesight may be housed in a building without elevator service, on the third or fourth floor.

The aged recipient with medical problems must hide the fact, or risk commitment to an understaffed, overcrowded, barren public nursing home, which (final irony) does not provide any continuous professional medical services.

Studies in psychology, sociology, biology, and many other disciplines have documented the deleterious effects of these conditions on individuals, families, and societies. Possibly the only solution to our staggering social problems lies in a fuller utilization of the findings of social science by the service administrations. Certainly chronic dependence, apathy, and a primitive, unfocused rage are inevitable by-products of a system which fails to recognize that everybody has the right to live.

I anticipate that some militants will regard any document produced by a former Department of Social Services employee as motivated primarily by the guilt feelings of the author. Perhaps others will assert that there are many compassionate con-

16

cerned workers employed by the Department who are sincerely dedicated to advancing their clients' welfare. To this latter argument, I can only point out that such workers generally resign after a year's services, at the most. Sensitivity, empathy, and social awareness are among the traits least esteemed by the Department in its employees. The sensitive and humane individual who aspires to a career with the Department must resign either his convictions or his employment.

The capacity for callousness, which at times seems to be almost a prerequisite for competence as a professional person, is reinforced by ignorance on the part of many social workers of the actual conditions under which the typical welfare recipient must live. It is this same naïveté which partially accounts for the highly vocal persuasion of some individuals that the poor are responsible both for their poverty and the powerlessness resulting from it.

The time is long overdue for both professional any lay people to re-evaluate this persistent stereotype in the light of the actual life style imposed by dependence on public assistance. If only one reader of the following case histories discovers something of the interdependence between poverty and the callousness, inflexibility, and insensitivity of welfare administration, I will consider my time and effort to have been well spent.

TWO

Growing Up on Aid to Dependent Children

As SOMEONE else once wrote, poverty is a personal thing. For Juana Miller, being poor meant watching helplessly while her thirteen-year-old daughter was subjected to daily physical assault. Today Angelica lives in a public psychiatric ward. She could return home, but the Department of Social Services refuses to give Mrs. Miller permission to move from her present neighborhood, and Angelica's physician, for obvious reasons, will not approve her return to the same environment.

To sixteen-year-old Luz Diaz, being poor meant sharing a two-room apartment, in an abandoned building lacking heat or plumbing, with her two-month-old baby, an ill mother, a

19

fourteen-year-old brother, and a seven-year-old sister, for two freezing winter months. Her baby has never had a bassinette, a crib, a christening dress, or a new toy. For two months Luz shared her "bed" (a brokendown sofa) with her baby and her brother. Luz had stolen the bedclothes from the back of a parked moving van.

For Anna Lopez, being poor meant having to choose between food for her son or payment of a utility bill. Because she chose the former, the family was without gas or electricity for three days. As a result, her sixteen-year-old son has decided to become a drug pusher in order to supplement the family's income from Aid to Dependent Children (ADC).

For Ileen Douglas, being poor means looking at her retarded son today and knowing that his condition is a result of a long-drawn-out period of semistarvation he underwent in his childhood. Once, Ileen's husband was a productive worker who contributed generously to the family's support. He lost his job and his sanity as a result of an investigation conducted by the Department of Social Services. The purpose of the investigation? To disqualify Ileen and her son from receiving ADC.

For Adeline Dulaney, being poor meant slowly losing her emotional balance as a result of trying to raise two children under unbearable conditions, and then being denied permission to move on the basis that she was "emotionally disturbed." Her children today live in a bleak public shelter. Denied permission to move from her unlivable beach shack, their mother abandoned them and disappeared.

This is an era of increased militancy on the part of all oppressed peoples. ADC mothers have long been in the forefront of the battles for more money, better apartments, and civil treatment from public servants being waged in Social Service centers across the country. Then general public is apt to agree with one U. S. Senator who called these angry mothers "brood mares on a stampede."

Few Americans have any real awareness of the actual conditions of life these families face. The few who are genuinely moved by their plight sometimes admit to feeling that "somehow they brought it on themselves." There has recently been a proliferation of scholarly studies on poverty and its effects on personality. These studies are couched in abstract terms and read, usually, by graduate students, social workers, and psychologists only. Very rarely are the effects of dependence on public assistance described in terms understandable to a layman, particularly to a politician. Yet daily the minds, bodies, and souls of growing children and their families are being destroyed by the administration of "aid."

Juana Miller's case history is by no means an isolated example of bureaucratic insensitivity. Nor is it an example of racial discrimination. Anyone in America today, forced to turn to public assistance for help in a crisis, will almost certainly face the callous disregard for the physical safety and emotional well-being of their children which today condemns thirteen-year-old Angelica Miller to remain in a locked ward, rather than allow her family to move to a safer neighborhood.

Juana and her family had been evicted from their apartment following the desertion of her husband. At the time of her application for ADC, she and the five children had taken temporary shelter with her sister. Angelica, previously labeled "emotionally disturbed" by the school system, reacted to this move by retreating into mutism. As a result, she had been suspended from public school, and Juana was directed to obtain psychotherapy for the girl. With no source of income, she could not possibly comply with this directive, so Angelica's school status remained in limbo.

Mrs. Miller's sister, Mary, though wanting to help, was in no position to continue providing shelter for these six guests. She was pregnant with her third illegitimate child (father or fathers unknown), and was on ADC herself. Juana was forced, as soon as her application was approved, to rent hastily a four-room apartment in a deserted section of Brownsville. Unknown to her, this area was under virtual siege by a roving band of adolescent boys, who periodically looted the buildings of the deserted section. Angelica quickly became sexual prey for this band. Juana appealed to her caseworker for permission to move, pointing out that she had found a better apartment. She was refused, on the basis that rent on the new apartment was ten dollars a month more than "allowable" by the Department.

Decent accommodations "allowable" are almost nonexistent in New York City, as Mrs. Miller discovered in a futile search. By this time she had restricted Angelica's movements to the point that she was never allowed out of the apartment. However, one afternoon Juana returned from apartment-hunting to find the lock broken on the door, and her daughter in a state of hysteria. Subsequent medical investigation disclosed that the girl had been raped that afternoon. She was placed in a psychiatric hospital, not only to soothe her immediate shock, but also in hopes of getting her back into school.

After three months, her doctors feel these results have been accomplished, but the girl refuses to re-enter the building where she was violated. A community action agency and the hospital social worker have both submitted emergency requests to the Department of Social Services for rehousing the family. Both these requests were denied because the Millers had lived at their present address less than a year, and had moved there under emergency conditions. Does this sound relevant?

Actually, the Millers' case record was in process for transfer to another Center when these emergency requests came in, and the worker and supervisor involved simply did not want to be bothered with change of address, change of family budget, and moving bill. (The Department manual prohibits transfer of problem cases. In actuality, however, the typical Center [with seventy to eighty cases per worker] regularly resolves its "problem" cases by transfer or "Code 8"—"can't locate.")

It is the Millers' profound misfortune that their human needs have not coincided with administrative convenience thus far. Perhaps when their new caseworker realizes that he, too, can transfer them if they are allowed to move outside his jurisdiction, there will be a more sympathetic reaction to their pleas.

Bureaucracies move slowly; "deadlines" for their clients can become grimly apropos. Particularly unfortunate are the victims of periodic ghetto burn-outs. The Diaz family was burned out of their third-floor walk-up on Christmas Eve, 1969. Since their apartment had already been scheduled for razing, the Department of Urban Relocation was contacted for help in finding them new accommodations. This agency acted quickly. They placed the Diaz family, in 10° temperatures, in an abandoned third-floor three-room walk-up without heat or plumbing. There were five people in this three-generation family. Margaret, the mother, had suffered severe injuries to her feet in escaping the fire, which made navigation of the stairs painful at first, ultimately impossible. Her daughter, Luz, had moved in with her mother when her common-law husband first locked her out, then disappeared with all their belongings. Luz had a two-month-old baby from this union. Ricardo, fourteen, and Juanita, seven, Margaret's other children, completed the family.

Luz had made formal application for ADC for herself and

her child a month earlier. She had not been given any help, nor any word on the status of her case. (The Department frequently disregards the legal time limit of four weeks for reaching a decision on new applications.) Margaret took her family to the Social Service Center on the 24th to apply for an emergency check for a week's food for herself and two children— Luz and her baby being nonpeople as far as the Department was concerned. The Center kept her there four hours, processing the check and paperworking the move to the new address. Consequently, the family did not arrive at the Urban Relocation office to pick up the keys to their new home until after 5:00 P.M. The office was locked, and would not reopen until the 26th. The Center was also closed through Christmas Day. The family, of necessity, spent that holiday in the misery and mess of their burned-out building.

On December 26, they finally settled into their emergency new quarters—a "temporary" shelter which would be extended through the two coldest months of the year. The caseworker who visited them discovered that Luz had stolen blankets and sheets from a parked moving van, in an effort to protect her baby. The baby was ailing, the clinic was seven blocks away, and Luz was carrying her there for daily penicillin shots, because she had no money for food, let alone carfare.

Ricardo, to save his mother's untreated foot injuries, periodically missed school to search for another apartment. The caseworker found, on the day of her visit, that he had finally located a replacement and gone to the Center to pick up rent and security-deposit. He found, after two hours in the Center, that his mother and the new landlord would both have to visit the Center before a check could be made out. The caseworker was able to convince the Department of the seriousness of Margaret's burns, and to arrange for Luz to pick up the check.

24

But it was too late. The landlord had rented to another family. The search for "acceptable-rent" housing was resumed by Ricardo, until he was detained in a juvenile correctional institute for truancy. During this time, before he was arrested, he and Luz and the baby had been sleeping on a sofa, while Margaret, somewhat obese, slept with Juanita in a single bed. Even if the beds had been new, which they were not, they would not have been comfortable for this many occupants. The apartment had no stove, nor substitute for one; yet the family survived another month and a half waiting for sixty cents per person, per meal, to be added to their budget.

With Ricardo's detention, the family found it easier to locate an apartment at the Department's level of rent. While this was only slightly more habitable and less hazardous than the Diaz' last two residences, it at least provided sporadic heat and hot water. An administrative fiat six months earlier barred any provision of funds whatsoever for furniture or clothing to a "pending" applicant, so Luz is once again eying unprotected moving vans. But even she will have trouble removing a bed unnoticed, which is the item she needs most.

As her child grows, its material needs will increase. Now that special grants for clothing and school expenses have been discontinued, mothers like Luz and Juana Miller will have to meet these needs from food money. Access to the public school's free lunch program is (like most of the benefits provided the insolvent) contingent upon public identification of the recipient. The children, at an age to disregard the long-range view anyway, regularly choose inadequate nutrition over social humiliation.

Success in school work requires acquaintance with the world outside the ghetto community. Newspapers, movies, trips to libraries, and television are impossible to provide on a welfare budget. Even when the school itself tries to extend the intellectual and emotional sensitivities of its students, the total deprivation and dependence characterizing these families renders the efforts fruitless.

One high school senior, Constance Hidalgo, was denied the simple pleasure of seeing her picture in the yearbook, due to the Department's delay in processing a grant to cover the cost. Mrs. Hidalgo submitted the request in October of the girl's senior year. Two visits to the Center and innumerable phone calls later, the caseworker processed the request in January. Her authorization sat in the Unit Supervisor's in-box for two weeks. This harried individual, in what was to have been the last step in the process, affixed his signature on the first of February. But a new edict had been issued—two signatures were necessary on this authorization now. The second functionary refused to sign until the caseworker made a second visit to the home to obtain additional information on the whereabouts of the missing father of one of the children in the Hidalgo family. This was done, and the information was obtained. The papers were again submitted for the second signature. Three weeks later, they were returned again to the caseworker with the notation that the client had failed to sign paternity papers (giving the Department the right to sue the father—if he could be located, in this case after an absence of fourteen years, and if he possessed anything to be sued for) again, for just one of her six children. This right-to-sue had to be signed by Constance's mother before the grant could be processed.

The caseworker, two days before the arrival of the family's semimonthly check, asked the mother to come to the Center. Mrs. Hidalgo did not have enough cash to transport herself and three preschool children to and from the Center ($3.20).

26

She had $1.10 left to feed the family on before the food check arrived, and $1.00 of that had to be spent on subway fare. (For some reason known only to the New York City Transit Authority, fares double past Broad Channel.) Nevertheless, Mrs. Hidalgo came to the Center, and Constance played truant to baby-sit.

Since the deadline for making payment to the school was now within five days, the mother requested an immediate "E" check, after she had signed the form. The caseworker, a well-intentioned trainee, was told by her supervisor that the provision of emergency checks in the absence of gross catastrophe was contrary to Department policy. Besides, now that all signatures were in order, the original authorization would be processed in plenty of time. The check, however, arrived at the Hidalgo residence two days too late, due, the administration declared, to an unexpected understaffing of the clerical section.

It was perhaps in anticipation of such bureaucratic dalliance that Anna Lopez had her nine-year-old son sent to New York from Puerto Rico without first obtaining her caseworker's approval. The boy had lived with his maternal grandmother in Ponce until the authorities there had removed her to a mental institution. The maternal grandfather, unable to provide day care while he worked, and not earning enough to provide long-term care for the boy, did provide his air fare to New York. Andrew arrived at J.F.K. Airport clutching a suitcase containing only a torn jacket and two sets of underclothing.

Anna duly notified her caseworker of Andrew's presence. The ensuing investigation by the Department of Social Services took four months, with no provision made for the boy's food or clothing in the interim. He attended school in a pair of pants and jacket several sizes too large, borrowed from the brother nearest him in size. His mother paid for his food by

27

withholding utility-bill payments. When she visited the Center with copies of the official shutoff notices from Con Edison and Brooklyn Union, she was curtly advised that since she had been using her aid money in ways other than the agency directed, she must now suffer the consequences of her defiance.

A neighborhood parish organization was able to arrange for an emergency loan sufficient to insure restoration of utilities to the Lopez apartment within the next three days. But in that time, Michael, sixteen, decided that never again would he or his family be solely dependent on the Department of Social Services. He has dropped out of school, and is now providing his mother and siblings with a second income through pushing heroin.

The child to whom such crises as utility shutoffs and non-receipt of checks are commonplace typically has diminished time and energy to devote to academic work. Ghetto schools regularly record decreased attendance on the first and fifteenth of the month, when missing public assistance checks necessitate that students baby-sit with their preschool siblings while the head of the household spends the day at the Social Service Center. In the innumerable instances when a check is delayed for more than a week, the school children attend school without having eaten breakfast, or dinner the night before. It is small wonder that they are described as listless and unresponsive on the playground and in the classroom.

Prolonged nutritional deficit can have tragic consequences. Joe Douglas is today irremediably retarded mentally because of nutritional deprivation suffered in his early adolescence. His parents, though not legally separated, were living apart, but Alan, the father, had been making payments of sixty dollars a week to his wife, Ileen, until a plant accident cost him the use of his right hand. Since he had only a fifth-grade edu-

28

cation, the work he found after his injury healed paid seventy dollars a month less than he had previously earned. At the same time, his aged mother had been stricken with cancer of the throat. The expense of her care coupled with the decreased income made the continuation of support to his estranged wife and child impossible.

Mrs. Douglas made application for public assistance for herself and the boy. After waiting six weeks she was advised, via form letter, that no action could be taken until she consented to bring formal charges of nonsupport against her husband. In the process of investigating Ileen's application, a form letter had also routinely been sent to Mr. Douglas' employer. He dismissed Mr. Douglas on receipt of the letter. What earthly purpose could have been served by bringing suit against him will never be known, for Ileen refused to consent. Consequently she received no support. Within the next two months Alan voluntarily committed himself to a mental hospital. Sickened by her first contact with the Department, Ileen vowed not to ask for help again. Unless neighbors shared food with Ileen and Joe, Joe went to school on an empty stomach. His apathy was noted by the school authorities, and he was transfered to a class for the mentally retarded.

Only after eviction (with confiscation of their personal belongings by the Department of Public Sanitation) could Mrs. Douglas bring herself to apply once again for public assistance. With her husband out of the picture for good, she was now eligible for help. She and Joe were given temporary shelter at a hotel located on Howard Beach, an area known to attract a heavy population of alcoholics and vagrants. While walking along the unlighted rural highway toward the hotel, Ileen was assaulted and robbed of the money the Department had given her to cover a week's food and rent. Penniless,

Ileen and her son spent the night in the entrance to the Broad Channel subway station. When they were discovered there by a subway patrolman the next morning, he gave them carfare to the Social Service Center.

Here a caseworker accused Ileen of having spent the money on alcohol, and refused to issue a replacement check. Mrs. Douglas borrowed one week's hotel rent from a friend, and she and Joe spent that week in the dingy, rodent-infested room, without food, before being formally accepted for ADC and re-housed in a one-room furnished walk-up.

The medical report filled out by the physician at the special school for retarded children where Joe was sent traces his mental condition to profound and prolonged nutritional deprivation. After the suspension (a clerical error) of his ADC grant on his eighteenth birthday, he was arrested for stealing food from a neighborhood grocery, and probably will not be allowed to return to school. Before the error could be rectified, Ileen was served with a dispossess notice, and again lived a week with no food money. A recommendation for Joe's official placement in a state institution is now pending before the court, and is expected to be acted upon within the month.

Any member of the ADC family, child or adult, discerns quickly that his future is limited. These people are subtly directed away from academic learning, at the same time that society condemns their lack of ability in this area. Any ADC recipient who attempts to improve his situation in life through education or specialized vocational training faces almost insurmountable obstacles. Gina Salas, whose education for a professional teaching career was financed by the New York State Department of Vocational Rehabilitation, was eventually forced to drop out of college because her request for carfare and baby-care fees was denied by the Department of Social

Services. The DVR, on Gina's behalf, urged a rehearing, emphasizing that Mrs. Salas lacked only twelve credits for a teaching certificate which would permit her to become self-supporting. During the three months that she and the DVR waited for an answer, Gina withheld payment to the utility companies to pay carfare and baby-sitter fees. By this time she was receiving student-teaching assignments, necessitating double carfares on certain days. By the time she received official word that her request had been denied, she was seventy dollars in arrears to the two utility companies. She made one last entreaty to the Center, in person. The caseworker promised to do what she could.

Another two weeks passed. One utility company tried to cut off her service, but Gina had had the foresight to remove her name from the mailbox, and the service man was frustrated for the time being. Finally the Department came up with a compromise. They would issue a two-party check to the utilities, and deduct the amount, in installments, from Mrs. Salas' food checks. In the very near future, some attorney will probably challenge the legality of this procedure. However that case may be decided, no judge need pronounce that it is morally and ethically indefensible.

Presently, Mrs. Salas and her daughter are receiving a flat twenty dollars semimonthly for food. Had she been able to complete her course of study, she would be contributing to society as a taxpayer and a teacher by now. Gina has become so depressed in her despair of ever getting off ADC that she has been referred to a nearby clinic for psychiatric help. But on forty dollars a month, she does not feel she can afford carfare on a continuing basis.

The occasional working mother among the ADC population fares no better than the prospective student. Though the De-

partment asserts that all employable recipients have an obliga-
tion to contribute to the family's support, caseworkers are reluctant to recommend supplemental finances for child-care
arrangements. Department regulations stipulate that a mother
working part time whose income is not sufficient to provide
day care for her child during the hours of her employment is
entitled to an addition to her allowance to pay a baby sitter.
Nevertheless, Carol James, having incurred a debt of fifty
dollars to her baby sitter after having taken a part-time job at
the telephone company, waited four months for the Department to approve the arrangement. This employment amounted
to fifteen hours a week, and Carol did not earn more than
thirty dollars in a single week. She had taken the job on the
recommendation of her physician, after consultation with her
caseworker. In urging her to take the job, the worker failed to
mention the fact that approval of baby-sitting fees generally
takes up to five months. Carol finally was able to expedite
matters by consulting a community action agency. The agency
finally prodded the Department into making a nonretroactive
addition to Carol's budget reflecting the cost of child care. This
was too late to be of any help, however. By now the baby
sitter had quit. Carol could find no other, and had to resign her
job.

Such examples of bureaucratic unwillingness to assist the
working mother could be enumerated indefinitely. Instances in
which a recipient's attendance at college or adult education
classes is considered grounds for discontinuance of assistance
are likewise legion. The Department is reluctant even to consider the part-time student's application, on the grounds that
he could conceivably be employed during the hours that he is
attending school.

This policy obviously disregards the limited employability

of the uneducated in today's job market. It would be more economical, in the long run, for the Department to finance a suitable educational or vocational plan for every member of an ADC family, than to shortsightedly and self-righteously insist that any employment, no matter how menial or unremunerative, is to be preferred to ADC maintenance.

A country which subsidizes extensive military engagements around the globe could perhaps more profitably subsidize the Gina Salas in this country. Certainly our national position and image, as well as our domestic stability, would improve if we stopped condemning people like her to a marginal position on the outskirts of hope and society.

All members of the family supported by public funds live with a basic anxiety as to whether or not their continuing needs for food and shelter will be met. The child growing up on ADC learns early that neither his parent nor his society is able to protect him or provide for him. He realizes early that adult authority is neither rational, benevolent, nor helpful. If an ADC mother like Marlene Williams retreats into a drug-induced psychosis to escape a reality experienced as overwhelmingly painful, society has no other alternative to offer than to place Marlene's children in a public shelter for children. In New York, this is Callegy Hall. The unbelievable conditions in this shelter were recently the subject of a series of articles in the Social Service Employee Union newspaper vividly depicting the dirt, overcrowding and squalor. Both the Mayor and the Commissioner of Social Services promised at that time to conduct a full investigation. Conditions there, however, remain abominable.

Abhorrent as the thought of placing children in his caseload in this institution may be, the caseworker with any particle of human compassion must take action for children living in

33

"homes" whose locus and composition change almost daily. Child placement typically consumes the better part of four months. In the Williams case, for example, the caseworker must initiate and follow up the placement process, while coping with eviction after eviction brought on by Marlene's addiction. She is adroit at finding friendly neighborhood vendors willing to cash the two-party rent checks issued by the Department, and friendly pushers to relieve her of the proceeds.

Addiction dulls both hunger and consciousness; Marlene is thus able to remain profoundly oblivious to the fact that her children are often without food or shelter. Sporadically, she shares her quarters with a series of transient male companions. The hastily occupied and just as hastily vacated dwellings the Department locates for the family are not noted for spaciousness or sturdy construction; consequently her children frequently witness sexual intercourse between Marlene and her current love. When she cast aside one of these men recently, he found a willing replacement in Marlene's fourteen-year-old daughter. The child's subsequent pregnancy finally accelerated the placement of all the Williams children. But the children are not physically secure in Callegy Hall, either, nor are they able to obtain there the psychiatric care a Department doctor alleges is necessary for them to overcome the shock of their former home life. White middle-class children can usually be placed for adoption, but children like Carolyn, Janice, Maria, and James Williams are not members of this preferred group. Undoubtedly they will continue the cycle of dependence, deprivation, and despair into the next generation.

Marlene, aiming for oblivion, was not traumatized by her children's daily exposure to rat bites, sexual harassment, and hunger. The ADC mother who remains in contact with reality, however, is spared no pang. She is confronted daily with evidence of her own inadequacy as far as preserving her children's safety and security is concerned. She must observe their hunger when checks are delayed. She must send them to school without coats or intact shoes, or face an unsympathetic truant officer. She must endlessly wage war against dirt in uncleanable rooms located in uncleanable neighborhoods, without soap, brushes, or brooms. At the risk of eviction, utility shutoff, or curtailment of future funds, she must furtively provide some sort of seasonal festivity at Christmas, Easter, Thanksgiving, and birthdays. Her children, she is helplessly aware, display a precocious sexual knowledge and experience as a result of exposure to prostitutes, homosexuals, drug addicts, and derelicts. Since infancy they have lived with such hazards as rat bites, hazing, bullying, and falls from unlighted stairways. With no telephone, neither police or medical protection can be summoned. The nearest public emergency room may be three or four miles from her home. After she arrives, she and the injured child must wait three or four hours for attention.

It is terribly easy to condemn a mother like Adeline Dulaney, who, when refused permission to move from her dilapidated and unheated two-room shack on the grounds that she was mentally unbalanced, disappeared, abandoning her two boys to the tender mercies of our mentally balanced public institutions. To imagine ourselves in this woman's intolerable position, receiving barely masked contempt from the agencies set up to provide material and psychological aid, is perhaps impossible. Yet the attempt must be made by all of us, professional or layman, executive or blue-collar, before we add our contempt to the already staggering burden of societal rejection placed upon women like Adeline and Marlene. Envision yourself and your children in overcrowded, dirty, rodent-infested, dark rooms, with every escape route blocked, with no

35

real assurance that even this shelter will not be denied you for some minor infraction of a rule. Imagine sending your children off to school knowing they have not eaten, knowing they are cold and ashamed, fearing for their physical safety in a world of society's rejects, fearing, too, that the check which finally arrives will be stolen from you, and knowing if it is that you may be accused of using it on alcohol or drugs.

Are any of us able to state honestly that in these circumstances we would not seek either physical or psychic escape as Adeline and Marlene did? We must see facts, not guilty rationalizations. We must replace fear with compassion. We must see that the struggle these mothers face is our fight too. Workers, students, and taxpayers, we have all experienced bureaucratic inflexibility at some point in our lives. Our oppression differs in extent, but not in quality, from that of ADC families. If our daily survival depended on an understaffed, inflexible, calloused bureaucracy, who among us would be secure?

THREE

Portraits of the Working Poor

PEDRO LOPEZ is thirty-two. His wife, Maria, is twenty-seven, a doll-like Puerto Rican woman who alternates between English and Spanish in speech. In the eleven years of their union they have produced five children, ranging in age from four to ten. For the past six years, Pedro has been employed as a die-cutter with a New Jersey firm. He commutes to work from Far Rockaway, getting up at 4:30 A.M. to do so. His working hours are from 7:00 to 5:00, with a fifteen-minute lunchbreak allowed. He works six days a week, receiving for these sixty hours a flat seventy-five dollars. His limited education and comprehension of English make more remunerative employment highly unlikely. So Maria works part time and weekends in a Manhattan supermarket, cutting and wrapping meat. She earns about sixty dollars a week after taxes, giving this family of seven a combined income of approximately $7000 annually—$3000 below the $10,000 the U. S. government estimates is necessary for a family of four in New York.

The Lopez family lives in an unfurnished, four-room walk-up located over a bakery on Beach 87th Street, for which they pay forty dollars a week rent. The four rooms consist of a living room, bathroom, kitchen, and bedroom. Rosa, seven, and Margarita, five, share a single bed in the bedroom. The older boys sleep in bunk beds in the same room, a makeshift partition separating them from the girls' bed. Miguel, four, still sleeps in a crib in the living room. There is no money for a new bed, nor space in the bedroom to accommodate it. The parents also sleep in the living room on a sofa bed which sags in the middle, and has a broken spring. There are three microscopic closets and one chest of drawers, the bottom drawer of which has come unglued. There is a seven-inch TV set, a gift from Pedro's brother. There is no public park or recreation hall within walking distance.

Though Maria Lopez tries to be an impeccable house-keeper, the apartment is infested with roaches and ants. During the evening, rats can be heard under the floors. To discourage these pests from surfacing, the Lopezes burn a light in each room all night, and pay about thirty dollars a month to Con Edison for this safeguard.

Miguel suffers from convulsions, and must attend a public clinic twice a week. Patrons of New York public clinics are not given appointments, nor are they assigned a personal physician. Maria and her son spend approximately seven hours a week waiting for, and vying with forty other families for, the attention of twelve physicians. Rosa has been diagnosed as mentally retarded and attends a CRMD class in the public school. Anthony, nine, has recently been suspended from school as a result of persistent truancy. School officials consider Mrs. Lopez "uncooperative" because she has failed to attend three conferences called by the principal to discuss her son's problems. Conferences, of course, are scheduled for the convenience of school personnel. Maria works from 9:00 to 2:00 on weekdays, with travel consuming another hour and a half. Despite union efforts, this chain of supermarkets does not grant part-time employees any sick or annual leave privileges. On the contrary, an employee who is absent two hours or more forfeits his entire day's pay. Loss of even $10 a day would be hard for the Lopez family. But the reason Maria failed to attend the school conference was that she was unable to read the notice sent her. Although she speaks English fairly well, she is unable to read it with any accuracy. The school board plans to refer both Anthony and Rosa to the Bureau of Child Guidance for testing, hoping to establish uneducability and disavow any further responsibility for their education.

A Spanish-speaking social worker employed by a neighborhood settlement house saw Anthony and his mother at the inception of the boy's school problems. He recommended that Anthony receive psychotherapy, and finally located a child psychiatrist who accepted Medicaid patients and had a vacancy between the hours of 10 and 11 A.M. But the doctor was located in Queens. Maria would lose $10 a week in wages, plus $2.80 daily carfare. The family budget would not permit such strain. Though originally well intentioned, the social worker closed the case with the notation that the mother was "unmotivated to help the child."

Pedro was recently absent from his New Jersey job for a week, due to an aggravated stomach ulcer. On the advice of a hospital social worker, the family applied for temporary supplementation from the Department of Social Services. In order

39

to file this application, Mrs. Lopez had to take the day off from her own job. In the course of the Department's investigation, a form letter of inquiry was sent to the children's school. Disregarding recent legal decisions, and without consulting his parents, the school provided the Department with the details of Anthony's persistent truancy and suspension. Good conduct reports on the other children were ignored by the Department, and although Anthony's behavior had no bearing on the family's financial status, his problems were regarded as grounds for rejecting the application. By the time the family received the rejection notification, Mr. Lopez, contrary to his doctor's orders, had returned to his job. Unfortunately, although Mrs. Lopez had arranged credit with the corner grocer pending the expected supplemental aid, she was five dollars short on the bill for rent. The landlord returned her check with a dispossess notice. Before an eviction was issued, Manuel, ten, took a week unexcused from school and got a job as a mechanic's helper by misrepresenting his age as fourteen. The family was thus saved from eviction, but owed fifty dollars to the grocer. Pedro is now working a second job as a store clerk evenings and Sundays, despite his health.

If ever a mother and father were motivated to provide for their children, Pedro and Maria certainly are. If ever a family adhered to standards of thrift, hard work, and frugality, it is certainly this family. Inasmuch as society seems determined to preserve the distinction between the "deserving" and the "undeserving" poor, the Lopez family would seem to have a clear priority for assistance. Yet all society's agencies—schools, welfare, health—failed to help.

This failure to perform the duties they were created for results in countless families like the Lopezes, precariously balanced on the edge of financial and emotional disaster.

40

Funds for a double bed, another bureau, but most of all for food, rent, and adequate clothing, allocated even temporarily, might have given Anthony the motivation he needed to attend school regularly. Had the Department been so inclined they might have helped the Lopez family find roomier, cleaner quarters. Sleeping comfortably, without the lights on, and with plenty of elbow room, might also have helped Anthony at school, to say nothing of Pedro's ulcers.

It is truly abhorrent that the Department of Social Services is able to deny such obviously needy and "deserving" families assistance on as flimsy a basis as one son's truancy. It is inconceivable that going without food (and very nearly shelter) can possibly be helpful in correcting his truancy. Nor will Anthony's irresponsibility be cured by Manuel's employment at the age of ten, nor Pedro's working two jobs in defiance of his doctor's slow-down order. It is shameful and unnecessary that black or Puerto Rican workers labor longer and harder for less money than their white counterparts.

While academicians, social workers, and politicians discuss poverty, families like the Lopezes and Hunters live it. No intellectual delineation, no matter how eloquent, can communicate the feelings of a husband and father who finds willingness to subject his wife and children to intolerable living conditions a prerequisite for receiving aid.

Such was the experience of Jim Hunter and his family. A piece-work construction worker with an airline, Jim had supported his wife and children adequately until the loss of his job three months before his application for assistance. He had been making $150 a week, plus occasional overtime, and his wife earned a little as a baby sitter. The rent on their three-bedroom apartment was $140. After Jim's layoff, the family floundered financially until forced to apply for aid. The week

41

after the case was accepted, Jim found new employment at essentially the same occupational level and rate of pay as his previous job. Because of the time lag before they applied for help, however, they found themselves two months' in arrears on the rent, and were served with a dispossess notice.

Since the payment of $280, even if strictly on a one-time basis, required the signature of the Director, and he discouraged submission of such requests, the caseworker tried to find them new quarters. The apartments shown them by two real estate brokers reflect better than words the low esteem in which the financially unfortunate are held in our society. One was a fourth-floor walk-up in an incredibly deteriorated section of Far Rockaway. The rickety stairway itself made it out of the question, for Mrs. Hunter's physician had attested in writing as part of the original application that her varicose veins allowed no stairs.

While the family was investigating the second dilapidated apartment, their seven-year-old son joined a gathering of adolescents on the street corner and was induced to take a drink of cheap wine. Dismayed at the thought of living in such an apartment and neighborhood, they refused this offering as well, and returned home.

There they found a notice giving them forty-eight hours to produce $280 or move. In desperation, and physically unwell, Mrs. Hunter came once more to the Center, arriving at 9 A.M. At 4:30 P.M. a unit supervisor condescended to hear her story. The supervisor then advised Mrs. Hunter that since the family had declined the housing located for them, they must forfeit their furniture to the Department of Public Sanitation and accept lodging in a "welfare hotel." Mrs. Hunter had become more and more agitated as the long day, a material part of her forty-eight hours, wore on, and at this helpful offer she became hysterical. A social service patrolman responded by forcibly escorting her to the door. Mrs. Hunter's physician directly attributes the loss of her expected baby to this trauma.

Next day a community action agency was able to exert enough pressure to bypass the Director's desk and contact the Commissioner, finally extracting a two-party check, payable to the landlord, for the accrued rent.

Families like the Hunters and the Lopezes are plentiful in our society, though underrepresented on public assistance rolls. The Department's unrealistic and rigid eligibility standards prevent some of the most needy from receiving aid. If Mrs. Lopez, for instance, were to quit her job in order to devote full time to her family (a step suggested by a hospital social worker to overcome some of the children's problems), the Department would accuse her of deliberately defaulting on her responsibility to be employed, and make this grounds for rejection of aid.

To the overburdened workers on Intake, constantly under pressure from field units to reduce the volume of investigations, any solution for the family, no matter how short range, is preferable to acceptance for public assistance (and consequent investigation). Applying this point of view, the fact that the Lopez family managed to get along in the past is basis enough to deny them help in the present. It is irrelevant that Mrs. Lopez is on the verge of a nervous breakdown from trying to keep house in an impossibly dirty and deteriorated building; care for five children, one mentally retarded, another chronically ill, a third emotionally disturbed; and hold a job at the same time. Only if she is actually committed to a state hospital can her family hope to receive help.

The children of such families are painfully aware of their debased status. Children of the working poor try to hide the family's dependence on public assistance by any means possible. It is not surprising that at the earliest possible moment they drop out of school to find work, and if unsuccessful, to find oblivion. These potential dropouts customarily receive little encouragement to stay in school from the Department of Social Services. In several instances, academically talented youngsters choosing to further their academic careers have instead been pressured to accept menial employment as a prerequisite for their families' continued receipt of assistance. Rosa Rodriguez' story is an example.

Rosa's father, José, has a chronic heart condition and has been unable to work since 1957. The family has been receiving assistance since 1964, when the relative who had been helping them died. Rosa had been a superior student all through school, in spite of the lack of space and privacy in her family's four-room apartment. She had been urged to attend college by all her teachers and guidance counselors. It was not until a year after she graduated, however, that a full-tuition scholarship from a civic organization made college a possibility.

The case supervisor for the Rodriguez family thought there was something wrong if a nineteen-year-old girl could attend college while her family was receiving public support. The entire family was called to a conference and presented with an ultimatum—either Rosa resume her sixty dollar-a-week job as a dishwasher immediately, or her father, mother, and two brothers would have to appear before a hearing officer to determine their continued eligibility.

Rosa, naïve, and secure in her past school record, could not believe that an impartial hearing in the higher echelons of the Department would penalize her family for her desire to attend college. Accordingly, she registered for her classes and waited for the hearing to establish her right to funds for textbooks

44

and carfare. She was stunned and angry when the hearing officer upheld the Center and suspended the family's aid, after listening for fifteen minutes to the case supervisor. Since Rosa was nineteen, one can only wonder at the reasoning behind this decision.

Rosa happened to be an extremely stubborn and resolute young lady, as subsequent events were to prove. She wasted no time in securing the services of a community action attorney. This lawyer told Rosa that he could probably get her family reinstated on public assistance if she were to live elsewhere while pursuing her education. She hurriedly made a desperate but futile search of her neighborhood for some family willing to give her room and board in exchange for her services as a housekeeper-maid. When all seemed lost, the Dean of Students at the university she planned to attend was able to arrange for Rosa to live in a student-operated co-op, in which ten hours of housekeeping a week was accepted in lieu of rent. The community action agency which had provided the lawyer free of charge also placed Rosa in a waitress job for spending money.

While this was going on, Rosa's family was served with a dispossess notice, and utilities in the apartment were discontinued. Mrs. Rodriguez herself tried to find work. Without carfare, and troubled by varicose veins, she didn't get very far. One week before the dispossess became final Rosa moved into the co-op, and her attorney accompanied her family to the Center to reapply for assistance. The Department saw fit to delay action until an eviction was issued. The supervisor explained to the caseworker that "perhaps if the family went without food for another week the mother would be motivated to increase her efforts to find employment." Since the Department has full medical records of both parents, clearly documenting inability to work, the supervisor's attitude is wholly inexcusable. The real motivation behind the stalling tactic was to force Rosa to give up her education and resume her contribution to the family's support. During the four weeks that the Department waited for Rosa to give in, her four-year-old brother was rushed to a public emergency room in a coma diagnosed as the result of not having eaten for two days.

The family went again to the Center, again accompanied by Rosa's lawyer. This time, he insisted on speaking to the case supervisor. After an hour and a half spent with the case-worker and the unit supervisor, the attorney was finally allowed to speak to the case supervisor on the telephone. The first fifteen minutes of this conversation consisted of a brisk exchange of threats. Then an agreement of sorts was reached. The Rodriguez family would be reinstated when, and if, the functionary directly above the case supervisor in the Center hierarchy accepted the fact that Rosa was unable to support the family by reasons of emotional instability.

Since the day Rosa moved out, her mother had been calling her every day, dramatically detailing the family's suffering. The community action agency, rightly or wrongly, had convinced Rosa that the city was responsible for caring for her family. She tried to explain this fact to her mother, but whether the mother understood or not, she was powerless to stop her entreaties. Rosa's next step was to cease answering the phone, and get her friends in the co-op to say she was out when her parents or the Department called. Torn between her desire to help and her need for education, she consulted a community psychiatric clinic. The psychiatrist counseling her reinforced her position to the extent where she could go on with her college career. The emotional instability required by the Department was, therefore, easily documentable.

But before reaccepting the Rodriguez family, the unit supervisor decided to make one last effort to persuade Rosa to relent. Since she would not answer the phone, they called the Dean of Students and asked her to send Rosa home at once because of an emergency in the family. Rosa came home and was persuaded to accompany them to the Center the following day. The unit supervisor insisted on talking to Rosa alone, while Rosa, by now discerning the nature of the "emergency," refused any discussion unless accompanied by her attorney. The elevated voices of Rosa, her family, and the supervisor attracted a patrolman, who insisted that Rosa leave Intake or face arrest.

Rosa gladly left, accompanied by her family. The unit supervisor then phoned Rosa's employer for information about Rosa's emotional condition and wages. Since Rosa was not applying for assistance, the legality of this action is highly questionable. Before the phone call, two form letters had been sent by the caseworker, asking verification of her wages. Both letters went unanswered. The employer was evidently allowing Rosa to fight her own battles with the Department. But this phone call, implying emotional illness on Rosa's part, occasioned her abrupt dismissal when she showed up for work that night. Despite the efforts of the Dean of Students and the community action agency, no other employment could be found for Rosa, and she was forced to leave school before the end of the semester.

The attorney, meanwhile, had appealed to the administrative office at 220 Church Street. That office finally got the family (except Rosa) reinstated, and a two-party check mailed to the landlord. Due to a recent change in policy, however, nothing could be done about the utility bill. The family remained without gas until they received their second semi-monthly check. The utility company, though not paid in full even then, finally restored service to the apartment.

Rosa is now working full time as an organizer for the community action agency. She and her new employer continue to be harassed by letters and phone calls from the Department. Her father and mother have again been threatened with suspension unless they bring legal action against their daughter for nonsupport. An almost identical case is now in a fair-hearing process. If the outcome is favorable to the client, Rosa and her attorney intend to bring suit against the Department for the constant harassment and intimidation suffered by Rosa's family for six months, and the forced termination of Rosa's education and previous employment.

The Department views with alarm the working poor's growing awareness of their legal entitlements. When the National Welfare Rights Organization began recruiting eligible working poor to apply for public assistance, the Department countered by drastically increasing the red tape necessary to process such applications. This discouragement, another form of harassment, daily turns away many clearly eligible families.

Most of the working poor were deliberately kept in ignorance of their rights to grants for clothing and furniture. When the NWRO and other community agencies began to demand their legal entitlements in these items, New York's "liberal" and "client-oriented" Commissioner responded by eliminating *all* such grants.

The Norton family was unfortunate in having its one double bed destroyed by fire one week after this decree. Their entire stock of bed linen was also destroyed. Mr. and Mrs. Norton had been sharing this bed with their six-year-old son, while an eight-year-old son slept on the sofa. When the bed burned, the two boys had to share the sofa, while the working member of the family joined his wife on the living-room floor, sans pillows, sheets, or blankets. The family slept this way for two weeks, until a community action agency was able to find a secondhand bed for them. Not surprisingly, Mr. Norton's job performance declined badly enough that he was dismissed. Before their application for public assistance could be processed, their utilities were shut off, and a credit company repossessed their dining-room table and chairs.

Similar disasters resulting from the abrupt cessation of the special grant could probably be enumerated indefinitely by social workers and antipoverty employees. Sound as the principle of the "flat grant" is in conception, the amount of money usually provided is simply not sufficient. A grant issued to the Nortons, for instance (if such grants had not been terminated), would not have covered the cost of a new bed and bedding. Installment plan purchase would have decreased their food budget to an unbearable minimum.

In order to do justice to these families, nationally agreed-on standards should be established for the articles of clothing, furniture, and household utensils which are needed to insure a certain minimal level of physical comfort. Under this system, certain poor families whose income is a few dollars above the maximum allowable for public assistance could nevertheless be eligible for special grants in certain times of emergency.

The National Welfare Rights Organization is doing an admirable job of acquainting eligible workers with their rights to financial supplementation. While the reluctance of city and federal bureaucracies to assist the community in recruiting eligibles to the NWRO is perhaps understandable, their refusal to cooperate with existing personnel of NWRO is inexcusable. New York's present Commissioner has stressed the "spirit of cooperation" which should exist between agency and community. In spite of this and other official pronouncements of good will, the Department's Intake workers view the NWRO's efforts as evidence of a diabolic plot. Any family able to qualify for assistance under the existing unrealistic standards is clearly in dire need. It is both cruel and unnecessary to place additional obstacles in their way.

In overhauling our welfare system, one clear priority should be the liberalization of present eligibility standards. Instead of a national standard of $2400 per year, local standards should be established which reflect the actual cost of living in that locality. The needs of a family fluctuate according to circumstances; no flat grant can in itself be sufficient to provide for every eventuality.

For the working poor, one frequent crisis not provided for under the recurring grant is the father's loss of a job. Aside from facing a wait of three to four weeks for assistance to begin (with the attendant inconvenience, embarrassment, and harassment), the breadwinner is gravely handicapped in his job search by a lack of funds for carfare, and suitable clothing. Job-hunting is an expensive proposition, even for the upper classes. It is unthinkable to expect that a man subsisting on a public assistance budget will be able to buy two or three daily papers, carfare to and from job interviews, clothing and personal grooming aids sufficient to impress a potential employer, without some addition to the family allotment.

A comparable crisis is the entry of a child into public school. Any mother can reel off a list of expenses incidental to public education—notebooks, rulers, crayons, erasers, etc. Self-esteem is injured if the child must wear the same outfit day after day.

The families described above are now the subjects of belated legislative and social concern. But society still, as always, neglects the most exploited members of the working poor. It is the *single* man or woman, without education, skills, or resources, who has been and is overlooked in legislative attempts to regulate wages and working conditions. It is these men and women who have been least affected by the victories won by the welfare rights organizations.

Applying for assistance, unless carrying a letter of referral from some city agency, these persons are quickly disposed of. "Go to Handy-Andy for day work and don't come back," is the refrain. In all probability, the applicant has already spent weeks haunting the corridors of Handy-Andy or some similar employment agency in search of one day's work. Quite possibly he has paid a placement fee for a job which turns out to be filled or nonexistent. Not aware of his right to have the fee refunded, probably lacking carfare back to the agency as well, he may try another agency or panhandle another day's existence. The Department must be aware of the exploiting these agencies perpetrate daily. Why, then, do they persist in referring the person back to the same agency he has already tried and found wanting?

If the applicant is undomiciled or facing eviction, he may be given a letter of referral to the Men's Shelter, an overcrowded and abysmal institution on East 3rd Street, where a population of rodents, lice, and bedbugs vies with the shifting human clientele. Physical abuse of patrons by guards is an everyday occurrence, also.

For a client like William Boyd, recuperating from a serious respiratory disease, the health hazards of such an environment, even for one night, could be fatal. Mr. Boyd had been drifting between various menial jobs. He lived in a cheap but clean and habitable hotel, and worked in a subway newsstand at the time

51

he became ill. The severe upper respiratory tract infection necessitated his absence from the job for five weeks. William's ilk have no sick-leave privileges; he forfeited not only his meager paycheck, but his future employment at the newsstand when he succumbed.

Williams used his last paycheck to prepay one month's rent to the hotel. A friend stole fruit and pretzels from vending stands to provide him with one meal a day. At the end of two weeks, he was taken in a semidelirious condition to a public emergency room. The hospital kept him two weeks, then discharged him with a letter of referral to the Department of Social Services, requesting that the agency find him another job. Not having an opening, the caseworker suggested that he apply for a City Civil Service position. Within a week he had passed a walk-in exam for a clerical position with the Department of Health at $110 a week. But city employees do not receive a paycheck until they have been on the job a month.

William's rent would expire in one more week. Though not excessive, the amount of rent required the approval of a case supervisor. This supervisor refused him a check, knowing it was a one-time request, despite William's desperate offer to reimburse the Department in the coming months. The caseworker, as disappointed as William, pleaded with the hotel management for a one-month delay in bringing his rent up to date. The hotel refused, firmly. The Department had been giving William a food check since his illness was discovered, however. He paid the rent with food checks, and went back to living on stolen fruit and pretzels. Disgraceful conditions in welfare hotels are well known, and it is not surprising that William would scrape any other possible way out of his dilemma.

The Department, of course, discovered that William's rent

had been paid, and where the money had come from. His caseworker was ordered to close his case immediately under Code 15 (failure to comply with Department policy). William now had to finish his first month of employment with no money for food or rent. Ironically, the supervisor on his new job, noticing his languor, suggested that he apply for public assistance.

Although this situation has humorous overtones, the outcome for William was quite tragic. A week before his first payday, he came home to find a padlock on his door, and his belongings confiscated by the hotel. He spent the night in the Emergency Assistance Unit of the Department, and was given twenty cents carfare and a letter of referral to the Men's Shelter in the morning. Here he slept three nights on the floor, in the presence of the aforementioned pests. Then his respiratory problem recurred to the extent that it warranted his emergency readmittance to the city hospital.

He has been a patient in an intensive care unit for the past two months. The city has terminated his employment on the basis that he fails to meet health requirements for the job. It took a hospital social worker to wring a check from the city for the two weeks that he did perform his duties. The social worker turned this check over to the hotel in order to reclaim William's belongings.

When and if William is released from the hospital, he will again be forced to apply for public assistance. Undoubtedly he will have a letter of referral from the hospital, so he will not be quite as helpless as other single applicants. This will probably prevent his return to the Men's Shelter, but the welfare hotel that is his only other alternative will be almost as unlivable. His chances of ever again becoming self-supporting (with the medical disqualification from the city blemishing his already-spotty employment record) are negligible. The taxpaying public are the ultimate victims of the Department's callousness in refusing him temporary help three months ago. William Boyd is almost certainly foredoomed to be a life-long recipient of Home Relief, or Aid to the Disabled.

The Department's policies toward clients like William Boyd often have the result of forcing these inarticulate and easily exploited men and women into involuntary servitude, often at less than the minimum wage. Department officials daily cut case loads by auctioning off individual members of its HR and ADC population to exploitive employers.

Margine Torres, a gypsy of twenty-one, for three months had been attending night classes in English, leaving her eight-month-old illegitimate daughter with her mother (an ADC recipient). The community action agency sponsoring these classes also did an excellent job of placing their "graduates" in jobs. Margine, already on ADC herself, found the twice-weekly carfare to the school an impossibility. It cost eighty cents each time she went. The caseworker to whom she applied for supplemental temporary help was faced with a dilemma.

To make an addition of $3.20 to a client's semimonthly budget, a worker must submit a detailed case history, which is then routed through five levels of administrative review. This process customarily consumes three to four months. In much less time than that, Margine would be forced to drop out of school. Yet she was doing well, and the caseworker was certain she would be placed in employment, once she gained command of the English language. But the caseworker knew that if Margine would come into the Center each day she planned to attend school, and fill out a special form, the case supervisor could then authorize carfare, one day at a time.

Margine gave her approval to this time-consuming aggra-vation, but the case supervisor would not. He argued that Margine, with the equivalent of a third-grade education, vir-tually no comprehension of either written or spoken English, and an eight-month old baby to care for, was nevertheless capable of full self-support, and should be stricken from the ADC rolls entirely.

By this time, the community action agency sponsoring the school, becoming aware of the students' problems, began issuing carfare to students on public assistance. If Margine had only been able to see into the future! The case supervisor was adamant in his refusal to grant her further aid if she per-sisted in going to school, so she took the job which the De-partment's employment advisor found her. As the supervisor had pointed out, there are jobs in New York City which do not require an understanding of English. Some factors asso-ciated with these jobs, however, the Supervisor preferred not to mention—they almost inevitably pay below minimum wage, are menial, offer no opportunity for advancement, and subject the worker to intolerable environmental conditions.

Margine began to operate a sewing machine in a tomblike unventilated basement plant without bathroom facilities, for ninety-five cents an hour. This was a few more dollars a week than ADC had been providing, true. But Margine now had daily carfare to reckon with, instead of twice weekly, and she either had to leave her baby, in its waking, most active hours, with her seventy-five-year-old mother, or, she thought, pay a baby sitter. What she did not know, and was not told—and may not have understood if she had been told, lacking English —was that the Department had the authority to grant baby-sitter fees to a person in her circumstances. But Margine was working now, and her case was closed amid administrative self-congratulations at having removed yet another dead weight from the welfare rolls.

Margine started working in the stifling Brooklyn basement during a week in which the mean temperature was 94°. Within a month, the baby at home fell down a flight of stairs and sustained a serious head injury. Margine began bringing her daughter to work with her, but her trips to the nearest public restroom (five blocks away) to change the baby aroused the ire of her employer, who dismissed her abruptly. When she asked for the money she had already earned, the foreman loudly threatened her with physical abuse.

A community action agency is now engaged in a battle with the Department to get Margine reinstated on public aid. The Department argues that Margine was never eligible for assistance, as she had failed to furnish the name and address of the baby's father. This man has threatened Margine and her family with physical violence if any information as to his whereabouts is given to the Department. In terms of police protection, Far Rockaway is one of the most neglected areas of New York, so Margine has reason to fear the consequences should the Department begin harassing him.

While Department officials and her community action worker argue the merits of her case, Margine, evicted from her beach shack, is now sharing two rooms with her mother, a sister, and the sister's two children. All of these residents, except Margine and her child, are ADC recipients. Margine steals five dollars a week from her partially senile mother. The Department is currently threatening Margine's mother with discontinuance unless she evicts Margine and her baby. It is hard to imagine where they would go. The Department's argument, that Margine is able to work, is fallacious. It is most earnestly to be hoped that future administrations will be motivated to find a more humane solution to the dilemma of third- and fourth-generation welfare recipients than the wholesale auctioning off of these people into an employment little better than slavery.

We could begin by recognizing and developing the untapped talent existing in nearly every rural and urban ghetto. In practically every welfare community, even the isolated gypsy enclaves of Far Rockaway and Coney Island, there are certain natural leaders. The courage, conviction, and dedication to justice of these men and women could well be emulated by some social service officials. These leaders, in daily defending the rights of clients like Margine Torres and Jim Hunter to decent living accommodations, decent food, and common courtesy from public officials, are performing a public service at least equal to that provided by the officially recognized agencies. Until government agencies become more humanized, society would be protecting its own interests by formalizing the status of these people, and providing them with adequate compensation for their arduous and often thankless work.

The poor must have flexibility, resourcefulness, and ingenuity simply to survive in their ghettos. The ghettos themselves provide uncounted opportunities for the exercise of these talents. Is there any reason, for example, why able-bodied, unemployed men and women should not be offered federally subsidized jobs repairing and cleaning up our decaying cities?

Since one of the perennial problems of the working welfare mother is the lack of adequate child-care facilities, why not utilize willing mothers and single HR women in a baby-sitting co-op or community-operated day-care center?

I am aware that private social agencies are making great

strides in uncovering and utilizing community talent in these and other ingenious ways. But to erase the blight of poverty, we must provide these workers with adequate financial compensation for their efforts. A community action worker who is tenacious and ingenious enough to slice through red tape to gain a Director's approval for a rent check to save a family about to be evicted should receive a salary at least equivalent to that paid the Department's caseworker. A neighborhood tutor who is able to turn a reluctant scholar on to the joys and advantages of education is doing a professional job, and should be compensated accordingly. This requires federal subsidization, in most cases. But to regard these potential workers as a limitless cheap labor pool would be a grave error.

Asking a case aide to perform the same duties as a college-educated professional for $130 less per week is a supreme affront. To coerce Margine Torres into working for less than the minimum wage because she lacks education, has an illegitimate child, and receives public assistance is a violation of her constitutional rights. It is also a negation of the ideals of justice and equality under the law upon which this nation was founded. The case aide (often a welfare recipient himself) doing a professional casworker's job at less than half his salary, cannot be blamed if he is less than totally devoted to his job. (Despite official utterances to the contrary, a great many case aides are doing essentially the same work as regular caseworkers. For the past year and a half the city has had a freeze on hiring new caseworkers. It is therefore probable that either the case aide or a clerk will be called on to make field visits, handle service calls, and perform other duties traditionally handled by the professional, while being accorded none of the professional's rights of tenure and salary.)

Can a young mother like Margine Torres, forced against

her will into an intolerable job, really be expected to give her best effort to that work? Studies by industrial psychologists have established that the productive worker is one who has had a voice in determining the conditions of his labor, and is able to see meaning in that labor. In our eagerness to transport recipients like Margine from relief rolls to pay rolls, we must remember that dead-end jobs will never substitute for the full rewards of meaningful and remunerative work.

Public opinion to the contrary, many of America's poor do labor. Someone once wrote that the chief disability of these men and women is that they work hard and get paid little. The work of Pedro Lopez and Jim Hunter, fully as much as that of J. Paul Getty and Nelson Rockefeller, preserves our society and keeps it functioning. Surely Pedro Lopez is a living monument to the qualities of diligence, self-reliance, and dedication to family that are said to be part and parcel of the American character. Horatio Alger to the contrary, neither the possession of these qualities, nor the lifelong labor of a man and his wife, have been sufficient to win prosperity or anything even approximating it. If society has failed these working poor in their expectations, it can at least recognize their rights as taxpayers and human beings to financial security, and to dignity.

Jim Hunter and Pedro Lopez have supported their families to the best of their abilities. That the level of support they are able to provide is inadequate is attributable to a host of sociological and economic factors, most beyond their control. To argue that an acquaintance with contraceptives could have prevented calamity is to beg the essential point. There is the reluctance of society to allow free distribution of information and devices. (Until 1966, provision of such information to unmarried women by caseworkers was expressly prohibited.

The same Commissioner responsible for this prohibition was the one expressing the most concern over "the alarming increase in ADC caseloads.") Contraceptives have been known to fail. Religious questions arise. A poor mother yearns for the "pitter-patter of little feet" as much as, possibly more than, a wealthy one. Indeed, large families (potential working hands) have long been seen as one way to rise out of poverty.

The essential point is that these families, with their progeny, exist, and cannot be wished away, or told "you shouldn't have. . . ." They must be provided with adequate nutrition, adequate housing, adequate clothing, and true job opportunity. These children and their families are entitled to the most sensitive and skilled help that society can provide. Financial supplement is the most vital component of that help.

FOUR

The Plight of
the Home Relief
Drifter

DANIEL MALDONADO is a vagrant. At present, his sole worldly possessions consist of one pair of pants, one ragged overcoat, and one pair of worn and undersized shoes. Daniel has at various times supported himself as a kitchen maintenance worker, a pretzel salesman, and a day laborer. Currently, he is existing by soliciting money from passers-by at the entrance to the Playlands Park subway station. Daniel has no fixed address. He is a sporadic visitor to the Salvation Army Mission in Manhattan. Occasionally he will forfeit seventy cents for a night's sleep on the subway, taking care to change trains whenever he catches sight of a transit patrolman. If you are a regular visitor to the Port

Authority Bus Terminal in Manhattan, you will probably catch sight of Daniel about once a month, catching an hour's shut-eye when police eyes are turned the other way.

Daniel has applied for day labor at various temporary agencies on Warren Street. On those occasions when his unshaven appearance does not immediately preclude his acceptance, he will pay a placement fee, for which he is sent to a businessman who is likely to advise him that the position has already been filled, or is no longer available.

Daniel has no living relative. He left a New Jersey foster home at the age of fourteen, failing to complete high school.

Daniel's circumstances, and his obvious incapacity for self-support, would appear to entitle him to immediate financial aid. About four months ago, having been advised by Salvation Army officials of the availability of public assistance, at 1:30 in the afternoon he stumbled into the district office closest to the subway station in which he had been soliciting money from passengers. Since he has no fixed address, he was advised that he could not receive aid from that office, but must apply to the Lower Manhattan Social Service Center.

Mr. Maldonado arrived at 11 West 13th Street at 9:00 A.M. the next day. After waiting three hours to be interviewed, he was subjected to a series of questions regarding his past, none of which were comprehensible to him. His sporadic employment had consisted of a series of one-day jobs in fly-by-night organizations. No records were kept, and there were no phone numbers which the Intake worker could call to verify employment. His memory failed to supply exact chronological order of his past jobs, or the exact dates on which he had held any of them. The nickels and dimes he had been begging were not accompanied by the names and addresses of their donors, nor was there any conception of total amounts "earned."

Daniel was advised that his inability properly to document his obvious need made his acceptance for public assistance impossible. The best that the Intake worker could do for him was to write a letter of referral to the Men's Shelter on East 2nd Street. Like most of New York's homeless population, Mr. Maldonado was already unhappily unfamiliar with this institution. It is questionable whether conditions at this municipal residence represent any appreciable improvement over such informal residences as the Port Authority Bus Terminal or the interior of the 14th Street Subway Station, which attract a transient population of homeless men like Daniel Maldonado in search of a night's sleep, free from harassment by the city authorities.

Despite the Welfare Department's allegations that its workers do not discriminate between the "deserving" and the "undeserving" poor, some approximation of middle-class respectabililty is almost prerequisite for the granting or continuation of financial assistance. Though the department manual lists financial need as the sole requirement for the granting of assistance, the agency daily and systematically discriminates against the most obviously needy members of the city's population. The vagrant such as Daniel Maldonado, whose appearance alone attest to his lack of friends or resources; the drug addict who has not yet been able to cut through the red tape involved in gaining admission to a rehabilitative project; the alcoholic resident of the Bowery; the unstable single woman without skills or relatives (turned prostitute in the absence of any other income)—all of these individuals, though clearly in need of financial and psychological rehabilitation, stand, under present processing policies, almost no chance of being accepted for either.

This clientele (less articulate and more easily intimidated) has not attracted proponents as readily as the better-organized and increasingly militant ADC population, whose deprivations are currently embarrassingly conspicuous. Consequently, it is easier for the Department to circumvent legal requirements in denying these men and women their right to aid. (One penniless gypsy women living alone in a beach shack scheduled for demolition was a periodic visitor to her district social service centre. Unfamiliar with any language but Hungarian, and unaware of her legal rights, she was each time routinely disposed of by the issuance of twenty cents' carfare. Eventually she concluded that there was no possibility of help from this source and ceased her visits.)

Daniel Maldonado and the other members of the transient population nightly haunting the corridors of the Emergency Assistance Unit at 220 Church Street are not skilled in self-assertion. Their encounters with middle-class society have conditioned them to be abjectly grateful for the meager crumbs of human compassion sporadically falling their way. Presumably this is why the ex-alcoholic Howard Mendleson, failed to report nonreceipt of his check, and spent fifteen days living on the charity of visitors to the public park near his rooming house. Having come to expect maltreatment from public authorities, he accepted the suspension of his sole source of food and shelter with the resignation common to those many members of New York's HR population, to whom poverty and powerlessness are facts of life.

Whereas there is a fairly specific series of steps legally prerequisite to closing or suspending an ADC case, and a fairly intricate appeals process available to the ADC mother, the Department's legal machinery is far less protective of the single dependent. The wide degree of leeway granted the city in dealing with this category of assistance, and the lack of federal reimbursement, result in a shockingly high percentage of eligible HR applicants being denied assistance. Once accepted, the Home Relief case can be routinely closed under Code 8 (can't locate) with only the most cursory investigation. In one instance, an epileptic woman's grant was discontinued after her emergency admission to a municipal hospital for acute pneumonia. The hospital failed to notify the Department of Social Services of Miss Alverados' admission to their facility. The young woman returned home after four weeks to find her furnished room rented to a new occupant, and her few personal possessions confiscated by the proprietor. The Department advised her that, due to her negligence in advising the center of her whereabouts, her case could not be reaccepted. Her only alternative, she was told, lay with the Emergency Assistance Unit. Applying there that evening, she spent the better part of ten hours waiting for service, only to be told that, since her case, was active at one of the city's regular social service centers, she was not eligible for emergency placement in the municipal shelter (the only service provided by that office at 220 Church Street). It was now 7 A.M. Miss Alverados had been sitting in the Emergency Assistance Unit since 9 P.M. the previous evening. Her last meal had been two days earlier, before checking out of the hospital. She had not been able to return to the hospital to pick up the medication ordered by her physician, without which she was subject to epileptic seizure. By now, she had exhausted her financial resources in carfare to and from the rooming house, the Social Service Center, and the Emergency Assistance Unit.

The best that the officials at this latter agency could do for her was to write out an authorization slip for twenty cents carfare back to the Social Service Center. Since the worker responsible for distribution of carfare did not arrive on duty until 9 A.M., Miss Alverados spent another two hours waiting. Finally arriving at the Social Service Center at 9:30, she found that the worker having responsibility for her case was in the field. Helplessly, she waited another hour and a half. Then the unit supervisor told her the agency could do nothing further to assist her, and that her current problem of being without food or shelter was hers to solve in whatever manner she could. This advice was overheard by a community action organizer who happened to be in the center and intervened on Miss Alverados' behalf. The insistence of this intermediary resulted in a series of phone conversations between the unit supervisor and the senior case supervisor at the Emergency Assistance Unit, both parties being resolutely determined to disavow any responsibilty for Miss Alverados. Negotiations were still going on three hours later, when Miss Alverados experienced an epileptic seizure.

This time, her condition necessitated a stay of three months in the same hospital from which she had just been discharged. Upon her recovery, she was placed by the Emergency Assistance Unit in the Women's Shelter on Broome Street—a placement strongly contraindicated, medically. Without constant medical supervision, Miss Alverados' physical and mental condition rapidly deteriorated until she became disoriented in both time and space. Losing consciousness one night in a Bowery alleyway, she attracted the attention of one of the groups of youths who prey on the helpless population of this section of the city. They set fire to her clothes. Her third hospital stay, seemingly permanent, is in the psychiatric ward at Bellevue.

The human tragedy of Elsa Alverados could perhaps have been prevented, had any of the many functionaries with whom she came in contact considered her as a person facing a crisis, rather than an economic liability. There are many men and women like Elsa, homeless and helpless, whose only sin is that their particular disabilities cannot be made neatly to fit into a category which is federally reimbursable.

To the extent that we remain unwilling to invest in the economic and human rehabilitation of these men and women, we condemn them to repeat the very pattern of behavior we decry. The alcoholic applicant is frequently instructed to rehabilitate himself at the same time that he is denied funds for food and shelter. The department is similarly noncomprehending of priorities in their dealings with drug addicts, real or suspected. These applicants are denied any aid, even carfare, until they have documented their affiliation with a rehabilitation agency. The addict in urgent need of immediate financial and medical assistance is typically unable to comprehend the many steps necessary to affiliate himself with such an agency. Even when willing and able to pass these tests along the way to his "cure," the addict faces urgent and compelling practical problems in the interim, such as where he is to live and how he is to eat, without funds. Neither the Department of Social Service itself, nor any of the projects to which he will probobaly be directed, are likely to provide much tangible assistance in these matters. If the addict turns in desperation to petty theft, beggary, prostitution, or any like illegal occupations, he will jeopardize his future acceptance for bureaucratic aid.

Most private agencies are, like the Department of Social Services, prejudiced against those very members of the population most obviously in need of help. By their unwillingness to extend their resources to men like Daniel Maldonado and Howard Mendleson, these agencies are themselves contributing to the social pathology they are supposed to cure. Being scorned by public and private charity alike, these men are doomed to be permanent residents of our Bowerys and Skid Rows.

For the unattached person, release from either a penitentiary or a public hospital is the most reliable route to acceptance for Home Relief. Such releases, whose financial and social status is attested to in writing by another city agency, are given priority in acceptance and housing over other applicants. These latter unfortunates must take up informal residence in Union Square Park or the Port Authority Bus Terminal and beg until their inevitable arrest for vagrancy makes them eligible for the city's largesse. The parolee is provided with formal lodging in one of the dungeonlike single-room-occupancy dwellings lining the Bowery and Times Square. It is hard to imagine a less rehabilitative or therapeutic environment for the mentally or physically ill. The "welfare hotel" is a frequent scene of homosexual assault and rape. The proprietor's one concern is that rent be paid in advance. Elevator service being notoriously unreliable in most of these buildings, the elderly or partially blind occupant frequently must navigate four or five flights of unlighted stairs to enter or leave his room. The incredibly lackadaisical standards of building maintenance and sanitation provide a fertile breeding ground for disease, rodents, and bedbugs.

The recipient who succumbs to any or all of these hazards can expect little or no sympathy from the city. During the Hong Kong flu epidemic of 1968, an efflicted HR recipient walked ten blocks from his rooming house to the Social Service Center without hat or overcoat to pick up an urgently needed Medicaid card. Once in the Center, he waited for two hours before receiving his card. Authorization of carfare having been rescinded that very week, the obviously ill young man was in a quandary. He could use the forty cents that represented two days' meals for carfare to the nearest public hospital, or postpone seeking medical aid until the arrival of his next check three days later. He chose the latter course, and set out for the long walk home, already limping from the torn shoes he had on, and bracing his skimpily clad body against the wind. His condition developed into pneumonia, and necessitated a month's hospitalization.

Equally unfortunate was the young releasee for a psychiatric hospital, who made formal request for rehousing after he had been assaulted by a homosexual group living in the rooming house assigned him. The nineteen-year-old's terror at returning to the scene of his assault, pathetic to witness, was dismissed by Department officials as a manifestation of his paranoia, and he was warned that further requests for rehousing would result in his immediate rehospitalization. Three days later, I found my caseload had been diminished by one, as the boy had not returned to the rooming house. At the age of nineteen, possessing only one jacket, one pair of pants, a pair of overalls, shoes, and a toothbrush, he has almost certainly joined the vagrants on the park benches and bus stations.

Unequipped emotionally as this young man is for the hazardous existence of the vagrant, eating and sleeping sporadically, always at risk of arrest or abuse, the alternative he faced in the welfare hotel was unbearable. Such an environment is totally barren and unstimulating. Such simple satisfactions as a movie or a magazine are not provided for in the HR recipient's budget. Neither is he allowed funds for new clothes, haircuts, or articles of personal hygiene; hence his appearance alone is enough to ban him from employment, not to mention his abject, hopeless vacuity. Although the condi-

FIVE

On Being Disabled
and Destitute in
New York City

THE VOLUME of notoriety received by the occasional affluent individual who makes fraudulent application for public assistance has been such as to convince the public that the welfare rolls are filled with able-bodied men who contrive to subsidize their reluctance to work through public funds. In actuality, New York City's own statistics reveal that only 3 to 5 percent of its recipients of public assistance are employable.

Under this latter category come able-bodied but temporarily incapacitated men like Orlando Morales. A lathe operator with a family of eight, Mr. Morales applied for assistance after a leg injury necessitated an indefinite leave of absence from his job. The family had lived from payday to payday when Mr. Morales was working; hence they were in desperate need by the time Mrs. Morales came into the Center in December to request emergency assistance.

She waited two hours, her two children crying from hunger, and submitted then to a long interview, apparently aimed at unearthing some nonexistent resource. Finally she was told to return the next morning with birth certificates for the eight children, as well as her husband's last six pay stubs. When she complied next day, she again tried to apprise the Intake worker of her need for *immediate* financial help. She was advised that no emergency check could be issued until another worker visited the family within the next two days. At this point, the Moraleses were receiving food through the generosity of an upstairs neighbor, and their landlord had given word that a dispossess would be issued within the next week if the rent was not paid. By the time the worker finally arrived at the Morales' apartment to verify the situation, a formal dispossess had been issued, and the family's money amounted to twenty-five cents. The upstairs neighbor had gone out of town. Mr. Morales was scheduled to enter the hospital for surgery on the following day, and the family did not have funds to transport him there and return. This family was informed by the worker that a check would be mailed "sometime during the next week," and that they "should locate another generous neighbor" in the meantime.

A community action group arranged for Mr. Morales' transportation to the hospital after having endeavored in vain to convince the Department of Social Services that the immediacy and urgency of the Moraleses needs justified issuance of an emergency check, and prevailed on the landlord to postpone his dispossess action.

74

Due to the heavy volume of Christmas mail, the Morales check, processed and mailed on the 22nd, had not been received by the family by the time of Mr. Morales' release on the 27th. Mrs. Morales, now on the verge of a nervous breakdown, borrowed forty cents from the same helpful group, to make another trip to the Social Service Center to demand an immediate emergency check. Arriving there, she was told that since two separate checks had been mailed (one for food and one for rent), nothing further could be done until these checks were either received by the Moraleses or returned to the Department by the postal service. Since carfare was no longer allowed, she had no way of getting back to her apartment, sixteen blocks from the Center. The caseworker's response to her plight was to tell Mrs. Morales that she could sit in Intake until the office closed at 5 P.M., after which she would be subject to immediate arrest. Mrs. Morales, with children to care for, could not risk this eventuality, and ended up walking home.

The family spent another day without food before the checks were returned as undeliverable by the post office. Once again Mrs. Morales presented herself at the Center, with four of her children, and waited three hours for a clerk to return from lunch to release the checks. As she finally received her money, she was advised by a worker to "for heaven's sake, get your name put on your mailbox unless you want this to happen every week." As a matter of fact, the checks had been mailed to the wrong address. The three weeks of totally unnecessary hunger and agitation undergone by this family were, as always, rationalized away as due to the negligence of the individuals involved, instead of correctly attributed to the insensitivity and incompetence of the bureaucracy itself.

It is inconceivable that Orlando Morales or any other man would subject himself and his family to this degree of humiliation were it at all possible for him to work. It is only dire and stark necessity which forces workers like him to rely on public assistance. Once accepted for financial aid, the temporarily disabled client often finds it all but impossible to obtain the special services and facilities needed to effect his rehabilitation. In theory, a man or woman receiving Aid to the Disabled is entitled to funds for medically verified needs such as special diets and carfare to and from scheduled clinic visits. In actuality, a worker who submits such a request for approval faces an exhaustive and time-consuming review of every aspect of the case record by as many as four functionaries. By subjecting every request, no matter how minor, to such excessive scrutiny, the administration reduces the possibility of bureaucratic ire toward the caseworker, and the caseworker reduces possible disqualification of his client for any assistance whatever. Most caseworkers, facing this not-so-subtle discouragement, simply do nothing to help the patient meet his needs for such devices as an orthpedic mattress or a prosthesis. A disabled person like Orlando Morales, then, will typically hobble three city blocks from the Social Service Center to the nearest subway. His caseworker has in all probability not been informed in her training sessions of the crippled or blind recipient's right to cabfare. Even if aware of his entitlement, he would probably be unable to process the multitude of forms and go through the three levels of approval required to administer these picayune funds, and still service as many as six other clients, all urgent, in the same day.

Similarly, a mother like Wilma Peters, temporarily incapacitated by an injury to her right arm necessitating a cast and two clinic visits a week, receives no aid from the Department of Social Services in housekeeping chores or in carfare, though she is legally entitled to both. Unless she discovers that she has a right to a housekeeper, she will (probably in disregard of medical advice) continue to do the cooking and cleaning for her family, awkward and painful and deleterious to her recovery though this may be. On "bad days" one of her children may take an unauthorized vacation from school to handle these chores.

Even when the disabled client is fortunate enough to have access to a community action agency able to advise him of his entitlements and act as his representative, the process of appealing the city's negligence before a State Fair Hearing Board and receiving a decision typically consumes three or four months. For the diabetic in urgent need of a special diet, the individual recuperating from a spinal operation in need of an orthopedic mattress, and for the asthmatic child choking for lack of a dehumidifier, three or four months is too long. The scales of bureaucratic justice are obviously unbalanced.

If state and city officials are sincere in their professed desire to restore these dependents to a condition of self-support, they should modify their procedures so as to provide for the medically prescribed needs of disabled clients such as Mr. Morales and Mrs. Peters promptly and expeditiously. The extent to which the city is willing to invest in these prophylactic measures may spell the difference between a productive normal life and chronic incapacity.

But in most city agencies there exists a very regrettable reluctance to provide services which would allow the mentally or physically impaired client to remain in the community. As a general policy, New York City's Department of Social Services would prefer to institutionalize the disturbed or defective client, rather than to invest in the facilities and personnel needed to maintain these people in their own homes. The emotional insulation developed by the majority of career employees in the Department allows them unquestioningly to regard removal to an understaffed, overcrowded public institution as the most economical solution to problems presented by the patient's presence in the family and community. A more humane worker typically spends up to six months trying to get authorization for theoretically available resources.

Fortunately for the cardiac patient, Arlene Surrey, and her twenty-one-year-old spastic son, a compassionate, trained housekeeper in her neighborhood volunteered to help her without pay until reimbursement could be arranged through the Department of Social Services. She cared for the severely retarded young man for six months without pay. During this time, the Department workers persistently tried to convince his mother to institutionalize him, and refused to make any commitment about funds. By this time, the altruistic housekeeper, technically employed by the Department, found it necessary to apply for assistance herself. Ironically, she was refused on the basis that she was employed full time!

Both Mrs. Surrey and the housekeeper have applied for state fair hearing to protest the unbelievably callous handling of this case. The housekeeper, of necessity, has found more remunerative employment, but she still donates one day a week to the Surreys. It is probable that Mrs. Surrey will soon have to decide between caring for her son at the expense of her heart, or committing him to a state institution; again at the expense of "heart."

Official certification of Aid to Disabled or Aid to Blind status carries certain benefits over and above those accorded the HR or ADC petitioner—namely, $2.50 extra semi-monthly, and freedom from pressure to accept employment.

Possibly for this reason, the process of obtaining such certification from the state is exceedingly complex and time-consuming. The multitude of medical forms and procedures cannot but be confusing to the semiliterate client, who will frequently disqualify himself by failing to keep appointments or return forms. The state, moreover, has established arbitrary and unrealistic standards as to what constitutes "disability." Not covered is a terminal cancer patient like Jade Wade. Despite the best efforts of a hospital social service team and his caseworker, this slowly dying individual was ruled ineligible to receive an additional five dollars a month for the few remaining months of his life.

Similarly, the alcoholic, unemployable without some form of specialized help, receives only enough to cover food and lodging. He is required to register with the Department's division of employment and rehabilitation, and must spend his food money on carfare to and from the fruitless job referrals they direct him to, in order to remain eligible for continued "assistance."

Though it has become fashionable in psychiatric circles to categorize the single recipient of HR as a "simple schizophrenic" or "character disorder," these disabilities are not recognized by the State Department of Social Services as entitlement to any financial aid above subsistence level, or to specialized medical services. Whether psychiatric disability is a cause or a result of dependence on public charity is debatable. It could be argued that the Department's insensitivity to the material and human needs of its petitioners is partially responsible for the large number of psychiatric casualties found among New York's recipients. The insecurity and anxiety experienced by a client whose check is consistently late cannot possibly be conducive to mental health.

When the check-processing machine failed recently, official reaction to this calamity in the lives of hundreds of clients was to make all those affected wait until the end of the week, when it was definitely ascertained that none of the checks existed. On Friday, most of the clients who converged en masse on the center were given emergency money for food and told that a replacement for the "lost" check would be mailed. However, the worker servicing one young mother of six children must have been either less charitable or more overburdened than most. She received sixty cents carfare pending issuance of a new check. Arriving home with this charity, and discovering a dispossess notice, she slashed her wrists with a razor blade.

The Department justifies its refusal to establish a home for a mother like Arletta Kennedy on the basis that she is not competent to maintain her own apartment. Since she has been diagnosed as an "ambulatory schizophrenic," that seems a reasonable argument. However, she currently is bringing up two children in a dilapidated, rodent-infested, unheated beach shack, in an almost totally deserted gypsy embankment. As aid from society, she receives a free weekly psychiatric appointment. If she is truly "ambulatory," she is, like any other mother, entitled to a decent and livable environment in which to rear her children. Our responsibility to all the Arlettas in our society extends beyond labeling their disabilities and segregating the most troublesome into the limbo of public institutions. If we hope to prevent incapacitation, mentally or physically, our attention must be directed to the unbelievably adverse conditions under which Arletta and other mothers and children dependent on public assistance exist twenty-four hours a day, seven days a week.

Instead, it sometimes seems that those most in need of help from public agencies receive the least. Had Josephine Rodriguez been given help in moving from an intolerable situation at the time when the need was acute, she would probably be self-supporting today. At the very least, her family would have remained intact, with a chance for growing to self-support. As it is, they are today scattered in various department shelters, and Josephine is confined to a public psychiatric ward, where her chances of ever leaving are minimal.

Mrs. Rodriguez and her six children had been put up in a single-room-occupany hotel after a ghetto burn-out had destroyed their apartment. During the family's brief residence here, the fifteen-year-old daughter was sexually molested by an intoxicated guest. The youngest daughter contracted bronchial pneumonia and had to be daily transported to a public emergency room. One of the boys was bitten by a rat and now required a series of tetanus shots. Mrs. Rodriguez suffered from high blood pressure and hypertension. Aside from urging her to find permanent accommodations for her family as soon as possible, the caseworker seemed unconcerned about her situation. As a matter of fact, when Mrs. Rodriguez was not en route to or from the public clinic (she had submitted two medical statements documenting the necessity of the visits but had not received any additional money), she was using every spare minute looking for an apartment. Many New York City landlords, unfortunately, happen to be prejudiced against both children and public welfare recipients.

After a community action agency interceded for Mrs. Rodriguez, the Department of Social Services contracted a real estate broker, who located a four-bedroom apartment. The condition and size of this apartment were such as to make it practically uninhabitable for a family of seven, yet their caseworker, reluctant to request another week's "hotel" rent, was insistent that the family move immediately.

The new apartment lacked dependable heat and hot water, and was infested with rats and bedbugs. After directing numerous unacknowledged complaints to the landlord about the lack of heat and falling plaster, Mrs. Rodriguez circulated a petition among residents of the building, which was subsequently mailed to the city Rent and Rehabilitation Commission. The landlord, previously oblivious to her existence, informally hired a band of teen-age boys to physically assault Mrs. Rodriguez and otherwise harass the family into moving again.

By a stroke of luck, her brother was able to find the family another apartment on the Lower East side of Manhattan. Freshly assaulted, and near hysteria, she visited the Social Service Center to request a month's rent as a security deposit on the new quarters. Now, as luck would have it, her former caseworker having resigned, her record had been transfered to another center. The worker in charge told her to go to the other center. The other center, however, had not yet received the "in transit" case record. After a wait there of four hours, she was told to come back in a week. She hysterically refused to leave. Police were summoned who took her to a neighborhood precinct. Here the woman pleaded for a police escort back to her old apartment, but they regarded her as an acute paranoiac, and gave her brother the choice of assuming responsibilty for her and her children, or allowing her removal to a psychiatric ward.

The brother, André Segura, lived in a two-room furnished apartment without bathroom facilities on the fringe of the Bowery. For the next month and a half, he shared these

quarters with Mrs. Rodriguez and her six children. Despite
André's almost daily phone calls to the Social Service Center,
his sister's next two checks were mailed to the old address.
No replacements were issued until they had been returned to
the Center. Although Mrs. Rodriguez was still legally responsible for rent at the old apartment, not having removed her
belongings, the new Social Service Center only replaced the
portion of her grant covering food. As a result, all of the
family's clothing and furniture were confiscated by the Department of Public Sanitation at the end of the month.

Also by the end of the month, the Department of Social
Services had decided that the Rodriguezes' living arrangements
were "not in the best interests of the children"—a conclusion
which would seem to be obvious. Instead of helping the family
obtain decent shelter and new furniture and clothing, the
Department directed its efforts toward placing the children
in a public shelter. Workers repeatedly visited Mrs. Rodriguez
at André's apartment, and tried to persuade her to relinquish
her children. To increase her motivation, her ADC grant was
illegally suspended.

The now-desperate mother turned to prostitution to secure
funds for her children's support. Nightly, she offered sexual
indulgence to sailors at Playlands Amusement Park. One
night she was picked up by the city police, and after two days
in the district jail, on the informal recommendation of the
Social Service Center, was transfered to a public mental
hospital, where she is still a patient. André had no alternative
but to consent to the immediate removal of the children to a
public shelter, where the five youngest still remain. Adoptive
parents for preadolescent Puerto Rican children with psychiatric problems are hard to find. The oldest, Yolanda, was
found to be suffereing from advanced syphilis. After her

release from the municipal hospital, she took up brief residence with a Gypsy, who left when she became pregnant. Now sixteen, Yolanda became another statistic in New York's ADC population.

Caseworkers will officially explain the behavior of Yolanda and her mother on the basis that they are "emotionally disturbed." If pressured, these same workers will admit that the family "needs help." Some workers, like the public at large, are conviced that "these people don't know any other way to live." Whatever its public or private views, however, the Department of Social Services has been extremely uncooperative with other agencies which are trying to assist handicapped clients to become self-supporting. Social workers and therapists and action agencies will testify that it is frequently impossible to effect a treatment plan for the low-income client without the cooperation of the Department. Joanna Lettimore's case illustrates this point.

Mrs. Lettimore came to the attention of a community casefinding agency through the anonymous reports of neighbors concerned about her frequent physical mistreatment of her two school children. An agency worker established rapport with her rather easily. Mrs. Lettimore was an extremely unstable person, tormented by fears of losing control and harming herself or her children. She readily admitted her inability to cope with the children rationally, but had not known where to turn for help. She was referred to a psychiatrist who accepted Medicaid patients. He was of the opinion that Mrs. Lettimore should be temporarily relieved of the burden of the children. At the same time, he was concerned that the family remain intact. This doctor was aware of his patient's eligibility for temporary homemaker service. He submitted a detailed psychiatric report with a formal recommendation that Mrs. Lettimore be provided with this assistance, pointing out that she was likely to harm herself or the children if not temporarily relieved of the full burden of their care.

Provision of homemaker services now requires the signature of the Center Director after five separate overburdened functionaries have scrutinized and passed on the entire case record. Mrs. Lettimore's domestic crisis unfortunately coincided with a citywide campaign by the Coordinating Committee of Welfare Groups to make more disabled recipients aware of their entitlements. The Department of Social Service, alarmed at this encroachment on their prerogatives, had imposed an unofficial but rigid quota system on granting aid of this nature. The social worker was unable to approve Mrs. Lettimore's unquestionably valid application because the quota on homemaker service had been already filled for that week (two cases). Theoretically, the full resources of the Department are available to any disabled client whose medical need can be documented. In actuality, this is not the case.

Honestly concerned, the social worker in this case next tried to get day care through the Bureau of Child Welfare. This agency was reluctant, arguing that Mrs. Lettimore should instead quit her job as a domestic. (This employment had no conceivable bearing on the home situation, as it only amounted to two days a week at hours while the children were in school. The problem was to care for the children during the hours the entire family was at home. Also, the psychiatrist had specifically stated in his report to the Bureau that it was only the brief respite occasioned by her employment that had prevented her complete breakdown.)

Ultimately, the Bureau of Child Welfare had no choice.

The same day the caseworker was writing a memo urging reconsideration of her situation, Mrs. Lettimore abandoned both children on a subway platform.

It has been argued that the Department does not itself create poverty and hence is not to blame for the deplorable conditions under which these people exist. True, the causes of poverty are complex and not within the province of any one agency to totally alleviate. But it *is* within the power of the Department to at least maintain the policy set forth in its manual. Interagency jealousies should not be turned against the client. Administrative policy should not veer with every wind that blows across the day's front-page news.

A family facing the incapacitating illness of its father needs financial assistance immediately. Temporary homemakers are crucial to disabled mothers. Cabfare is a necessity to crippled recipients. The retarded son of Arlene Surrey is entitled, both legally and morally, to a more hopeful future than deterioration in a bleak state institution. All these aids the Department is already empowered to use against poverty, but the attitude of administrative personnel denies their full impact.

The fact that present funds are inadequate must not be used to excuse the Department's unwillingness to utilize available funds to the fullest extent. The tragedy in the lives of the Rodriguez children is a direct result of the Department's failure to fulfill its legal mandate to assist its recipients in finding decent and adequate housing. Joanna Lettimore and her children could have been rehabilitated except for the arbitrary and illegal quota system, which might not have been in effect a day later. Society is the loser when potentially contributing humans are shuttled into institutions permanently, to avoid a temporary expense. The psychiatrist who took time to treat Mrs. Lettimore as a human being, and more

86

time to write up her case, is frustrated and less likely to bother about the next applicant. The caseworker in the Department who tried to further Mrs. Lettimore's case is presumably sadder and wiser. Measured in both economic and human terms, the cost of the Department's insensitivity and indifference to these people, and to society, has been incalculable.

SIX

The Bitter End: Growing Old in the Poorhouse State

SOCIAL WORKERS and physicians acknowledge that the aged poor are in need of extra support and understanding. Most aged, just by the natural course of the years, become socially isolated. They outlive their friends, or are forced by loving families to move away from them. Those who have loving families retain at least familial social relations, but many children in today's pressured world find it impossible to take on the burden of an elderly parent. Married children often have four elderly parents to consider, as well as their own growing family. Not only does increasing knowledge of geriatrics add to longer life (therefore more elderly population), but the increased mobility of the younger population (distance and divorce), decreases the possibility of home care for the aged by a concerned relative. The diminished physical and mental capacities of the elderly also cry out for extras, in time, money, and sympathy. But the public assistance they receive, in the words of one of the theme songs of the welfare right movement, is "not enough to live on, a little too much to die."

The aged client often lives in one of the incredibly bleak and deteriorated single-room-occupancy buildings, nicknamed "welfare hotels," described in an earlier chapter. The aged recipient is even more susceptible to the innumerable safety and health hazards found in such a building. His failing eyesight makes the navigation of four or five flights of unlighted stairs dangerous to himself and to other occupants. With advanced age comes lowered resistance to arthritis, rheumatism, and respiratory infections. These and other illnesses—some potentially fatal—are annually contracted by aged recipients who live in the inadequately heated SRO buildings during winter weather. During the summer, excessive heat and the inadequate ventilation of most of these rooms may combine to produce a medical emergency for the cardiac or asthmatic recipient.

A large percentage of the aged poor suffer from some diagnosed physical malady requiring continued medical care; but the services they receive from our public clinics are fragmented, indifferent, and conducted on an assembly-line basis. A client frequently spends up to ten hours a week in a overcrowded public clinic, waiting for routine medical services such as renewal of a prescription. There is little continuity of

90

contact between the patient and any one physician. One aged client recited her medical history to five different doctors in the course of six visits for treatment of an acute urinary disorder. Like recipients discussed in previous chapters, the aged poor individual with medical problems gets no carfare allotment. He either pays from his food budget, or does without the clinic visit. One client, with weekly visits prescribed to three different clinics, regularly ran out of food money by the end of a week. The rare sympathetic worker she complained to might occasionally "lend" her a dollar pending arrival of her next check. This was a decidedly nonprofessional solution, and frowned on by the administration.

The aged client's wardrobe typically consists of one or two dresses, either too large or too small, and a few tattered articles of underclothing. Such items as winter coats, hats, and properly fitting shoes are rarely found in their closets, or upon their persons. Inadequate clothing contributes immeasurably to their isolation, and not just during times of inclement weather. One woman hid in her single room for two months after ripping her one functional dress.

Aged recipients living on the upper west side of Manhattan frequently congregate in the waiting room of the Port Authority Bus Terminal. They prefer this atmosphere to the barrenness of their rooming house, but they must maintain perpetual vigilance for the police.

Those living near Rockaway Beach until recently had access to the benches lining the Playlands Amusement Park as their socializing point. Park authorities removed the benches to discourage these nonpaying patrons of Playlands.

Formal organizations providing social activities for the elderly as a rule do not welcome the financially distressed applicant. Truly, these are the clients nobody wants, nobody understands. Perpetually shrugged off, most of these people are trapped in a wall of loneliness and isolation.

Astonishingly, however, The New York City Department of Social Services has a preference for the aged recipient. In the words of one case supervisor, "they keep out of sight." Physical problems usually preclude the elderly client's participation in protest demonstrations, such as marches or weekend occupations of public buildings. Perpetually insecure, the average old age assistance recipient is hesitant to endanger his sole source of support by demanding increased benefits.

One aged client who did not "keep out of sight" was Annette Garing. Sixty-two-year-old Annette and her husband, sixty-seven, had been living in a small but adequately furnished apartment until Mr. Garing's sudden death from a stroke. Public assistance had supplemented his allotment from social security. After the sudden death of her husband, Mrs. Garing began experiencing severe depression. Her physician arranged for her temporary hospitalization in a public psychiatric ward. This doctor had taken unusual pains to maintain communication with the city Department of Social Services, so that the latter agency must have been aware that this hospitalization was a short-term measure only. The hospital's social service as well made three separate phone calls to three different Department functionaries, endeavoring to explain that it was essential that rent payments on her apartment be continued.

Nevertheless, the Department of Social Services closed Mrs. Garing's case, and her personal belongings were confiscated during her hospitalization. The only basis that I could discern for the senior case supervisor's reluctance to maintain Mrs. Garing's home in her absence was that Mrs. Garing had come into the Center a month previously, accompanied by a community action lawyer, and refused to leave the building until a replacement was issued for her lost semimonthly check. Mrs. Garing paid for this unusual act of self-assertion with the loss of her living accommodations, clothing, and furniture.

Upon her release from the hospital Mrs. Garing reapplied for assistance, and was given lodging in a building which was subsequently declared uninhabitable and condemned by the city building department. This residence did not provide heat or hot water, and was overrun by rats. The room occupied by Mrs. Garing had just been vacated by another "guest," who had been injured by a piece of falling plaster, seriously enough for hospitalization. The room was on the third floor. The elevator had been out of order for over six months, so this crippled and partially blind woman had to walk up and down the stairs if she wanted to escape the oppressive atmosphere of her room. This residence, contrary to its contract with the Department, did not provide bed linen or towels to its guests, and cooking facilities were largely inoperable. Nevertheless, Mrs. Garing received no restaurant allowance, nor grant for her personal needs.

The neighborhood in which this house was located was as depressing and dangerous as the interior of the residence. Though Mrs. Garing was generally afraid to leave her room, one oppressively hot evening she thought to escape the stifling confines of her four walls by walking one block to a street vendor's stand. On the way, her purse was snatched, containing all her cash. Ten of the fifteen dollars stolen were owed for rent, overdue because of a delay in mailing the allotment. She attempted to explain to the landlord, but he was unsympathetic and verbally abusive. She then came into the Social

Service Center seeking permission to move to new quarters. The same supervisor responsible for her plight, refusing to sign authorization for the move, responded to her request with the words, "every other client has been robbed at least once, why should she be any different?"

Mrs. Garing was afraid to contact the attorney who had helped her before, for fear of jeopardizing her continued receipt of food and shelter. Her case was transfered to another center shortly after she was refused permission to move, and before the building was condemned. In all probability, she now lives in another single-room-occupancy building in another dreary neighborhood, entirely alone, or has become a permanent resident of a public geriatric ward.

Deplorable as these single-room-occupancy buildings are, most elderly recipients prefer them to the only other alternative—permanent incarceration in a public hospital or nursing home. Department functionaries recognize this and use the threat of removal to the Neponsit Home for the Aged as a disciplinary device. Thus, Olga Santachurchi was told that she must either turn her mentally handicapped daughter out of her room (and back into the prostitution she had recently left), or risk eviction and commitment to a public hospital.

The daughter, Lucia, has been in and out of state schools for the retarded. Not being able to get a job, she had applied for public assistance twice, and twice been rejected. So she became a prostitute, until a police raid on "her" amusement park put a stop to that. A third time she applied for assistance, and again was told she was ineligible for Home Relief (for the same reason cited in a previous chapter—her former employers could not be contacted to verify her "employment"). An applicant denied HR is not allowed a fair hearing. Instead, he is permitted to appeal the decision in writing and receive an "administrative review" of his case by a state functionary within thirty days. How he survives this period is his concern. Lucia cannot write, so she could not apply in writing for this review.

But she was more fortunate than most of New York's unsuccessful HR aspirants. Her mother, Olga, was receiving Old Age Assistance and living in a public housing project on Beach Channel Drive. She took her daughter in and shared her meager subsistence, rather than see her go back on the street. Things went well until the New York City Housing Authority discovered the arrangement. Eviction proceedings were instigated and a copy of the charges against Mrs. Santachurchi was mailed to the Department of Social Services. The mother was called in for an urgent conference with her caseworker and a unit supervisor. At this "discussion" the supervisor "suggested" that since Mrs. Santachurchi could not manage her funds properly, she would be better off in a nursing home. (As a matter of fact, Mrs. Santachurchi had never even requested a special grant, and had managed very well on the pittance allowed her.) She is customarily exceptionally mild mannered; however, she became quite agitated at the insinuation that she was incompetent and required hospitalization. Quite heatedly, she asked what else she could have done, since Lucia had no job skills, no place to live, and had not been able to receive help after filing three applications. The supervisor's answer was that she should recommit her daughter to the same state school from which she had signed her out at the age of seventeen (after learning that the girl was being routinely beaten).

As it happened, Mrs. Santachurchi did not have to take this step. Lucia tactfully disappeared from her mother's room and set up an informal business at the intersection of Broadway and 49th Street in Manhattan. But her mother feels "useless," is moody and depressed since Lucia left. The Housing Authority now claims she is an incompetent housekeeper and a menace to the harmonious environment of the Beach Channel Project. She has been subjected to two "counseling sessions" with agency employees. The gist of these sessions has been that by voluntarily committing herself to a public hospital, she can spare the agency the time and expense of evicting her. Sufficient psychiatric evidence to commit Mrs. Santachurchi to the Neponsit Home for the Aged is also being acquired. Ironically, the same system which forced Lucia to turn to prostitution to support herself now wishes to institutionalize the one person willing to help her.

For the average Old Age Assistance recipient, living on public assistance imposes severe and frequently unbearable emotional burdens. A client like Olga, who becomes disturbed while bearing these burdens, is customarily committed to a public institution on the basis of a ten-minute scanning of his case record by a Department doctor who, in all probability, has not even met the patient. Department officials will frequently magnify any evidence of approaching senility in one of their OAA cases, in order to hasten his or her removal to an institution, thereby closing the case. Doubtless many of the elderly men and women currently incarcerated in the Neponsit Home would be able to get along in the community if provided with an adequate wardrobe, accessible and efficient medical care, and carfare to and from a recreational program. The tragedy is that these old people, perhaps the most in need of help, though least articulate in their need, receive so little from society. As long as they remain out of sight, in isolation, the Department assumes they have no "problems" requiring "services." It is only when a client like Olga Santachurchi or Annette Garing succumbs to the psychic or physical hazards of a barren existence that the Department imposes "services," in the form of peremptory psychiatric examination and commitment, after which, presumably, they again have no "problems" requiring "services." The institutions to which they are committed provide only minimal physical security. Life thus becomes a seemingly endless wait for death and public burial on Ward's Island.

The DAB (disabled, aged, legally blind) classification represents the city's latest attempt to cut its budget at the expense of those clients most in need of specialized services. One overburdened and understaffed clerical unit is assigned sole jurisdiction over all DAB cases in a center. Few of these clerical workers have had training or experience in social work. Working with the alternately irritable or inarticulate aged client requires a high degree of sensitivity and skill on the part of the professional social worker. To expect untrained clerics (hired, of course, because they will work cheaply) to provide the sort of relationship these clients need while simultaneously wrestling with forms and procedures, is to be entirely unrealistic. Not only the DAB clients but the clerical workers also are the victims of this lack of realism.

The supervisors of these clerical workers are even less willing to authorize emergency checks or initiate case consultation memos than their social service counterparts. Consequently, the DAB client wishing to move from an intolerable building, the diabetic in need of a special diet, the person with multiple medical problems traveling to several clinics a week, and others with special needs all can expect a cursory "no" to any requests for help.

Theoretically, clients covered by DAB are to be advised of the availability of extra services (such as individual or group counseling, or provision of a homemaker) at the time of their acceptance for financial assistance. As mentioned previously, however, these theoretical services are rarely provided in fact. Few of the clerical workers are even aware that financial counseling or day recreation programs exist for these clients' use. Another vital fact rarely shared by the clerical worker (presumably by Department deliberate policy) is that an applicant ineligible for regular financial grants may nevertheless be eligible to receive surplus food. Four months after the formal initiation of DAB (September 1969) an informal survey of the clerical unit revealed that only two out of the nine workers were aware of the existence of the surplus foods program, and one of the two was under the mistaken impression that only recipients of public assistance were eligible for this food.

With one untrained clerical worker per two hundred DAB clients, any meaningful service becomes an impossibility. The client, instead, must be thankful to receive a routine service such as renewal of a Medicaid card if he only has a wait of five hours.

Another serious complaint against the DAB system is that it often deprives the aged client of his one "friendship." The elderly man or woman without living relatives, isolated in a menacing neighborhood, frequently looks forward to the twice-yearly visit of his caseworker with a childlike eagerness. Now that DAB has relieved the caseworker of this drain on his time, the aged client is deprived of even this tenuous tie to the outside world. True, welfare rights groups have taken the position that such visits represent an invasion of privacy. And in most cases ADC, HR, and some DAB clientele experience

98

these visits correctly as a policing of their private life. But for the client in circumstances described above, a visit from an understanding friendly caseworker may be the one thread supporting his sanity.

For an isolated OAA recipient like Margaret Gomez, abandoned by her one illigitimate child and living alone in a squalid one-room beach shack, the loss of her one occasional visitor was undoubtedly traumatic. After her case was trans-fered to DAB, she became an almost daily visitor to the Social Service Center in search of the caseworker whom she had been told would not be visiting her again. Only an extremely lonely person would spend eighty cents a day in carfare simply to talk to another human being for ten or fifteen minutes. Mrs. Gomez' former caseworker realized the old woman had no other friend, and didn't mind granting her a few minutes' time each day. Inevitably, however, the service work-ers responsible for making a daily tally of visits and reasons for visits to the center noticed the oddity of Margaret's daily presence. With characteristic understanding, the supervisor arranged for the caseworker to be in the field or in dictation whenever Margaret appeared.

By this time the old woman had formed a new relationship. A young man in Intake "paper-bagged" his lunch and habit-ually ate behind his desk. Margaret usually arrived about noon without having eaten, and the young man occasionally shared his meal with her. The administration of Intake as well as the service unit administration were both alarmed. It was decided that Margaret should be ignored until 5 P.M., at which time a patrolman would escort her to the subway.

The original caseworker, against administrative decision, resumed home visits to Margaret's beach shack once a month. Undoubtedly she will be subject to severe disciplinary action should her generosity in providing this old woman with fifteen minutes of companionship a month be discovered. Not only the client but the caseworker must exercise considerable ingenuity in solving the problems of the dependent aged. Administrative callousness and insensitivity almost destroyed (and may yet) Margaret Gomez in the same manner as Annette Garing and Olga Santachurchi were destroyed.

If we hope to formulate a more humane social policy, we must realize that the most urgent need of the indigent aged is for a secure and adequate income. Money alone will not solve the complex problems facing our senior citizens. Isolation, rejection, manipulation and inadequacies of medical care and housing require social and legislative action. However, an adequate income would permit the aged client to provide for himself to a much larger extent, with corresponding increase in self-esteem and purpose. As things stand, the client frequently cannot afford toothbrush, comb, or razor. Understandably, he hesitates to expose himself to society. The two leading reasons given by clients for failure to attend scheduled clinic visits were: (1) The fact that in a choice between food and rent or carfare, there really is no choice; (2) Shame at appearing in public in torn, dirty, nonfitting clothing. The Department of Social Services' scale of "allowable" rents should more nearly correspond to the actual cost of finding decent accommodations in a city facing a severe housing shortage. Only financial investment can provide comfortable and adequate housing, and prevent some of these isolated, sometimes partially senile, men and women from spending their final days on a public geriatrics ward where, if they can pray at all, they pray only for death.

Most of these people, even the partially senile, are salvageable if given meaningful help and support from society. Tragically, even those like Olga Santachurchi, who have demonstated an ability and a desire to be of some use to others and themselves are frustrated and cast out by the very agencies society has empowered to provide for her and her offspring's support. The time is long past due for these agencies to demonstrate that they are at least capable of the same compassion their clients exercise.

SEVEN

Epilogue

Rosa Rodriguez, Marlene Williams, Annette Garing, Daniel Maldonado, and Joanna Lettimore—these and other fictionalized names used throughout this book represent real human beings. All of these people, whatever their limitations and failings, had the potential, if not to become fully self-supporting, at least to make some contribution to the welfare of their fellow human beings and to society. All of these individuals have been demoralized, diminished, and dehumanized by their encounters with the Department of Social Services.

Why must it be so—that the very agency set up to rehabilitate the poor and the powerless contributes so materially to the perpetuation of poverty and powerlessness? In this book, I have tried to the best of my ability to illustrate (without in any way indicating the many compassionate men and women who are also working in social service centers across the country) the callousness and inhumanity of many welfare officials and workers. Along with bureaucratic insensitivity, I

103

believe American public opinion must also stand indicted. In the eyes of the general public, the man or woman dependent on public assistance is seen as shiftless, irresponsible, and unwilling to work. Ironically, one result of this persistent and inaccurate stereotype has been to cause those "most deserving" in bureaucratic eyes—the most diligent, responsible *working* person whose earnings are simply not sufficient to provide for his or her family—to be among the most reluctant to ask for the help to which they are legally entitled. And this very reluctance often leads them into such financial chaos before they finally ask for assistance that they, too, end up by fitting the stereotype.

Not everyone has the time or inclination to become actively involved in the continuing fight against oppression now being waged by America's poor. But we can all exercise compassion and restraint in our judgments. Given the same unfortunate set of circumstances, any one of us could, like Jim Hunter and Juana Miller, find ourselves in the position of being unilaterally ordered to move, with our families, into substandard, overcrowded, rodent-infested housing in an urban or deserted rural ghetto.

Any mother like Olga Santachurchi or Arlene Surrey who has faced the financial and emotional problems of caring for a disabled child can imagine her own reaction if she were forced to relinquish her offspring to a bleak public institution as a prerequisite for receiving financial support.

Any worker like Pedro Lopez and Orlando Morales who has spent a lifetime of long and diligent labor, with little compensation, in order to provide for his family, can empathize with these men's feelings after applying for temporary help in a medical emergency, and then seeing his wife and children go without food, clothing, and sometimes shelter, while this assistance is denied or delayed for incomprehensible reasons.

Given our own sudden illness or incapacity, with no relative willing to assume the burden of our support, we could see our own children condemned to spend the remainder of their childhood and adolescence in the bleak and hopeless Callegy Hall, or some like public shelter.

Now, perhaps more than at any other time in recent history, we must replace rhetoric with empathy and true understanding. As I write this, Congress is debating a "welfare reform" bill which would bar any assistance whatever to single men and women (like William Boyd and Elsa Alvarado), force ADC mothers with preschool children into menial employment at below minimum wage, and impose stringent and unrealistic nationwide eligibility standards, which would strongly discriminate against the marginal worker. I do not think I am dramatizing when I state that, if this "reform" measure actually goes into effect, it will mean that men, women, and children will literally be allowed to starve as a matter of public policy.

America's poor have long been regarded as expendable, partly because of their lack of organization and their apathy— an apathy bred of a lifetime of repressed rage in the face of seemingly invincible oppression. As a result of organizations like the NWRO and affiliated local antipoverty groups, the poor are finally becoming aware that they need no longer passively accept substandard housing, police brutality, inferior education, and inadequate public assistance. Nor need the more fortunate sit helplessly by and allow our government and public agencies to destroy people who, whatever their race, religion, or financial status, are, in the last analysis, human beings, even as we ourselves are.

105

Five important things nonmilitants can do in their spare time to help America's welfare recipients are:

(1) Write, however briefly, to your congressman, senator, and other public officials, and express your opposition to the Nixon administration's proposed "welfare reform" bill.

(2) If you can, send money—as little as one dollar will be sincerely appreciated—to the Poverty Rights Action Group, 1418 H Street, Washington, D. C. The money is used to publicize the problems of welfare recipients, provide transportation for recipients from all over the country to and from D. C. to testify at hearings on poverty and welfare, and provide emergency help for recipients in situations in which the Department of Social Services fails to fulfill its legal requirements in providing food and shelter.

(3) Read:

> *The Poorhouse State,* Richard Elman (Pantheon, 1966)
> *Regulating the Poor,* Francis Piven and Richard Cloward (Pantheon, 1971)
> *One Family,* Nancy Sirkus (Little, Brown, 1971)
> *Still Hungry in America,* Robert Coles, M. D. (World, 1965)

These are a few of the best books on the subject. Your librarian can probably suggest others.

(4) Vote for officials who are pledged to work towards raising public assistance benefits to a level commensurate with the actual cost of living in the twentieth century. Ask all local candidates to give attention to

the problems of welfare and unemployment in your local community.

(5) Last, but possibly first in importance, when confronted with a friend or relative who is of the opinion that welfare recipients are dependent through choice and not necessity, try to acquaint him with the facts of life on public assistance. Try to abolish the stereotype he carries in his mind. You can refer him to this book, or to the others listed above. Enlightened public opinion is the first step toward changing public policy.

A 23R
6-10

Mi O X R